THE
EVERYTHING.
GUIDE TO
COMMODITY TRADING

Dear Reader,

If you are a typical investor, you will get much out of this book. You will learn the best way to make money buying commodities ETFs (exchange traded funds), how to build your own commodities portfolio, and how to evaluate commodities-based mutual funds. Some real differences between this book and others are that I've both bought and sold commodities as an investor and as a dealer. I've worked as a gold and silver bullion dealer in the past. Because of this, I've had the rare chance to hold 1-kilo bricks of pure 24-karat gold in my hands and stack them up in a safe. I've heaved 5-gallon pails filled with 100-ounce pure silver bars out to the backseat of investors' cars while they paid cash for the metal at the counter. Add real experience with scrapping out gold-filled pocket watches, sterling silver, and sorting old pennies to trading paper investments such as leveraged oil and copper ETFs and commodities currencies, and I've brought you the real honest-to-goodness knowledge and enthusiasm that I bring to my own investing and trading.

Welcome to the rewarding world of commodities trading!

David Borman

Welcome to the EVERYTHING® Series!

These handy, accessible books give you all you need to tackle a difficult project, gain a new hobby, comprehend a fascinating topic, prepare for an exam, or even brush up on something you learned back in school but have since forgotten.

You can choose to read an Everything® book from cover to cover or just pick out the information you want from our four useful boxes: e-questions, e-facts, e-alerts, and e-ssentials.

We give you everything you need to know on the subject, but throw in a lot of fun stuff along the way, too.

We now have more than 400 Everything® books in print, spanning such wide-ranging categories as weddings, pregnancy, cooking, music instruction, foreign language, crafts, pets, New Age, and so much more. When you're done reading them all, you can finally say you know Everything®!

QUESTION

Answers to common questions

FACT

Important snippets of information

ALERT

Urgent warnings

ESSENTIAL

Quick handy tips

PUBLISHER Karen Cooper

MANAGING EDITOR, EVERYTHING® SERIES Lisa Laing

COPY CHIEF Casey Ebert

ASSISTANT PRODUCTION EDITOR Melanie Cordova

ACQUISITIONS EDITOR Ross Weisman

SENIOR DEVELOPMENT EDITOR Brett Palana-Shanahan

EDITORIAL ASSISTANT Matthew Kane

EVERYTHING® SERIES COVER DESIGNER Erin Alexander

LAYOUT DESIGNERS Erin Dawson, Michelle Roy Kelly, Elisabeth Lariviere

Visit the entire Everything® series at *www.everything.com*

THE
EVERYTHING®
GUIDE TO
COMMODITY TRADING

All the tools, training, and techniques you need
to succeed in commodity trading

David Borman, Author of *The Everything® Guide to Day Trading*

Avon, Massachusetts

This book is dedicated to all those who have struggled to finish a manuscript on time: the early mornings, the late nights, the cups of coffee, and the endless frozen pizzas.

An Everything® Series Book.
Everything® and everything.com® are registered trademarks of F+W Media, Inc.
Published by Adams Media, a division of F+W Media, Inc.
57 Littlefield Street, Avon, MA 02322 U.S.A.
www.adamsmedia.com

ISBN 10: 1-4405-3600-7

ISBN 13: 978-1-4405-3600-7

eISBN 10: 1-4405-3622-8

eISBN 13: 978-1-4405-3622-9

Printed in the United States of America.

10 9 8 7 6 5 4 3 2 1

This publication is designed to provide accurate and authoritative information with regard to the subject matter covered. It is sold with the understanding that the publisher is not engaged in rendering legal, accounting, or other professional advice. If legal advice or other expert assistance is required, the services of a competent professional person should be sought.

—From a *Declaration of Principles* jointly adopted by a Committee of the American Bar Association and a Committee of Publishers and Associations

Many of the designations used by manufacturers and sellers to distinguish their products are claimed as trademarks. Where those designations appear in this book and Adams Media was aware of a trademark claim, the designations have been printed with initial capital letters.

*This book is available at quantity discounts for bulk purchases.
For information, please call 1-800-289-0963.*

Contents

Acknowledgments

I would wholeheartedly like to thank my editor Lisa Laing, who gave me first, second, and third chances with the completion of this book. I would also like to thank all of the people who are out there skimming through investing books, and who stumble upon mine and decide to buy them. Lastly, I'd like to thank my mother, Cynthia, who spent the final weeks of this book in "combat mode," both of us loading up on frozen pizzas and diet root beer, right to the end.

Top 10 Things Every Commodities Investor Should Know

1. Buy gold on Monday mornings: Gold prices usually go down on Monday mornings.

2. U.S. pennies dated 1982 and older are 95 percent copper and are worth about 3 cents each (at this writing).

3. A 3× leveraged crude oil ETF will go up 300 percent more than a regular oil ETF.

4. Central banking websites are the best sources of inflation information.

5. Inflation, money supply, and a good economy make commodity prices rise.

6. When economic news is bad, gold and oil will go up, while silver and copper will go down.

7. Crude oil, gasoline, heating oil, and gold prices are seasonal.

8. Consider investing indirectly with stocks and mutual funds if you are a conservative investor.

9. Consider trading futures or buying private placement offerings if you are an aggressive investor.

10. Know that an investment cycle lasts seven years or longer and investing in commodities puts you at the beginning of one of these seven year cycles, allowing you to ride the price wave to its peak.

Introduction

COMMODITIES HAVE BEEN ESSENTIAL to the financial well-being of people and economies for thousands of years. Since the days of the Egyptians, grains were bought from other lands and shipped to the cities for the citizens to bake bread. Gold was used on the mask of King Tut, and copper was used on the tips of the king's swords.

Later, gold and silver were used as money, which continues to this day. Grains, wool, and cotton have been grown in areas that had fertile soil, and today some countries such as New Zealand earn a great deal by shipping these raw materials to other countries that need these commodities.

Commodities have been brought to light again in this day, and this is mainly due to the economic conditions that were brought about since the banking and housing crisis of late 2007–09. Due to the near collapse of the world's economies, many of the largest central banks of the world went to extraordinary measures to insure the recovery of the fragile banking system and household economies.

Some of the measures taken were rapid decreases in base interest rates, with some rates being brought down to near zero percent. Other measures taken were the ramping up of the money supply in the United States, Japan, and Great Britain. These measures were called such interesting names as "quantitative easing (QE1)," "quantitative easing 2 (QE2)," "QE3," and "Operation Twist."

These elements alone would lead you to believe that it is a good time to buy commodities and have a commodities position in your portfolio. If you take this information and add to it the fact that the economy is just teetering at the end of a recession and just about to exit the past slowdown, well, then you have an excellent time to get into commodities trading!

This can be good if you are ready and prepared for the upcoming rise in prices. It may be that you would like to accent your overall investment portfolio to include a higher percentage of gold and oil ETFs with a base amount invested in a broad-based commodities mutual fund.

Your financial advisor or financial planning software may be suggesting that you have a mixture of stocks, bonds, cash, and alternative investments. By definition, commodities are an alternative investment, and you may decide to shop for and include a CTA—commodities trading advisor—on your list of investment help.

You may also like to try the oldest form of investing in the land—buying gold and silver ingots and coins. You may like to hold the coins in your hand and feel their weight. Finally, you may like to try your hand at "treasure hunting" and look for scrap gold-filled and 14-karat gold jewelry and know how to estimate or accurately judge the actual gold weight (AGW) of the item, only to then buy it at a price that is less than the value of the gold!

The ideas for commodities trading and investing are endless. Commodities are here to stay, and the time for them to become more and more expensive is just starting now, as raw materials are at the beginning of a full investment cycle. This means that while all forms of investments take their turns riding the wave in popularity and profitability (starting with bonds, then moving to stocks, and then to commodities) the normal seven year (or longer) full upward swing in prices is just beginning for commodities. This is due to the banking and worldwide monetary and economic factors that happened beginning in 2008–2009 with the housing and banking crisis and then the worldwide recession that followed. Why not take the time to get to know how to buy and sell gold, oil, copper, grains, and industrial metals, and add them to your portfolio?

Now is the time. There are still good deals to be had for the astute trader and investor.

CHAPTER 1

Why Invest in Commodities Now?

In this first chapter, you will learn the reasons behind why commodities experience rapid price growth. You will also learn that if history repeats itself, you can take the price of everyday goods such as coffee, corn, oil, and gasoline and fairly assume a rise in these asset prices that can easily surpass those of stocks or bonds. You will learn the basics to the price of raw materials: supply and demand. This chapter sets the stage for the concepts that are presented throughout the rest of this book.

Unlimited Growth, Limited Resources

"Oil reaches $175 a barrel; gold tops $3,500 an ounce!" Are these tomorrow's business headlines? Could it be true that you will be living in a time when you have to pay $12 for a gallon of gasoline and $7 for a small cup of regular coffee? Some say that if the economic growth of the world continues that these will soon be some of the average prices of the products you consume daily.

With the potential unlimited growth of the world's economies and the ability for central bankers to create an unlimited supply of the world's paper and electronic currencies, there still remains the fact that there is a limited (sometimes *very limited)* supply of the world's natural resources. Some of these natural resources are consumables such as foodstuffs; some are used as inputs in further processed manufactured goods; and others are an age-old method of storing wealth in nondestructible forms. Either way, ***commodities*** are physical goods that are grown or mined and must be shipped and stored. This puts them in a special class of investments. This also puts you in a special time in history: a time of worldwide growth and worldwide money expansion. These combined factors add up to an ever-increasing demand and price increase of the class of investments called commodities. You can choose to ride the wave with the increasing scarcity of commodities and reap healthy rewards as you do so.

Wouldn't it be nice to invest in such a way that you can capture some of the price increases in commodities? Wouldn't you like to insulate part or all of your entire portfolio from the effects of the massive increases in money supply that have been pumped into the world's economies? Wouldn't you like to record capital gains when you sell off your holdings of gold and silver as they reach their ever increasing price levels?

If you answered *yes* to any of these questions, then this book is for you. By reading this book you will learn the whys of commodity investing, including why now is the time to include a portion of your overall investments in commodities such as energy, agriculture, and metals. You will also learn how commodities can be considered an alternative asset class, and how historically commodities have had returns uncorrelated to the stock markets.

You will find answers to the questions: Are commodities a good investment for you personally? If so, how do you go about building up a commodities portfolio? You will learn how to use ETFs, futures, managed futures, electronic spot trading, and even the physical commodity itself as investment tools.

Once you make the decision that commodities are for you, you will then learn how to use fundamental and technical analysis to know the best times to invest and build your positions, as well as how to read developing news for signs of the future prices of your commodity positions.

You will learn about crude oil, gold, silver, and copper trading. You will also learn about the food commodities including coffee, cocoa, and sugar. You will learn the ins and outs of getting into the market, including indirect methods such as mutual funds and commodity currencies. Lastly, you will learn the most basic method of shopping for and buying the metal commodities in their actual physical form such as gold coins, silver bars, and copper ingots and coins. Additional information will be given on how to determine the actual gold weight (AGW) and actual silver weight (ASW) of gold and silver jewelry and other items found at antique shops and second-hand stores.

Growth in Emerging Markets

One of the reasons behind commodity price increases is the rapid growth rate of the world's emerging markets. Markets in developing countries such as Brazil, China, and India are growing at rates of 6 percent, 7 percent, and even 10 percent or more per year, year after year. This growth rate means added demand of finished goods that the Western world would consider normal; that is, there is a huge demand for finished products such as cars, scooters, and higher-quality homes. These finished goods require raw material inputs such as iron, steel, copper, and lumber. This equates to an added demand not only of raw materials but also of the energy commodities that go into the fuels to get the raw materials to the manufacturers.

Adding to the overall commodities demand is the fact that, in addition to the growth in many of these other countries, there also comes a higher level of inflation in the home country. This brings an increasing demand for commodities that can serve as currency alternatives, which act as protection from paper money that might be worth less in the future, or as savings accounts for the increasingly richer population. This means an added number of people are buying precious metal commodities such as gold, silver, platinum, and palladium. This increased demand is felt worldwide, especially during times of the year when the local customs are to buy for wedding and holiday gifts.

FACT

The Chinese New Year in mainland China or the marriage season in India can lift the prices of gold and silver as much as 20–30 percent in a few months. Historically, these higher price levels of gold and silver remain until they fall back a few percentage points in the slow months of August and September. The prices of gold and silver get pushed up farther again starting in October and ending in April of the following year.

The price increase of precious metals commodities such as gold and silver can act as an upward commodity demand/price spiral. The increasing price of gold and silver brings added wealth to the holders of the metals, which in turn spurns demand for more cars, scooters, and houses. If the increasing price of gold brings enough wealth, there is an increased demand for other goods, including finer clothing (affecting raw wool and cotton prices), better and more food products (which affects the price of food commodities such as wheat, corn, and cattle), and heavier usage of fuels in larger and more expensive cars.

Do not make the mistake of underestimating the potential demand and consumption of the world's developing nations such as Brazil, China, and India. There is so much demand for these countries to grow and modernize that it will take years of development for them to slow down and reach the growth levels that are seen in the United States and Western Europe. This growth demand will be adding to the raw materials demand for years to come. The net effect of all of this current and potential demand is one means for you to get in on an opportunity and gain high returns with commodities investing.

Supply and Demand and Commodities Investing

The basic question of any form of investing is, Where does the price base come from? In other words, who or what is establishing the price of the item that is to be invested in? If the item were to be bought for an investment, then you would need to know what has the potential to move the price up, and therefore give you the opportunity to sell the item in the future at a higher price (thereby making profits on the investment).

With this in mind, it helps to get a grip on what moves the price of the commodities. Basically, the prices of commodities are directly related to supply. Somewhat. To put it simply, the more of a good that is in the market in relation to the amount of demand there is of that good, the less the price of the good in the marketplace. Turning that around, if there is a higher demand for a good than there are supplies of that good, then there will naturally be higher prices paid for it.

Starting with Commodity Price Intervention

As far back as the 1950s there was a great quantity of commodities such as coal, steel, copper, tin, oil, and natural gas. Because of this, prices were low. In addition to this glut of supply, some commodities had their prices regulated by the government. There have been times in the past (and possibly in the future) that the U.S. Congress has regulated the price of food commodities and of some energy commodities. In the 1950s the price of natural gas was managed by the U.S. government and regulated to keep its price low.

How did regulations act to suppress the natural gas industry?
This government intervention prevented the oil producers of Texas, Oklahoma, and other western states from developing the equipment to get the natural gas they produced to the market. The prices were so low that there was very little development of the natural gas industry during these years. In fact, there was very little effort to keep an adequate storehouse supply of natural gas and other energy commodities.

As you will learn later, the glut of natural gas and other energy commodities slowly found itself widdling away until there wasn't a surplus. In fact, the combination of the underdeveloped natural gas storage capacity and the style of U.S. cars to have bigger and less fuel-efficient engines led to a kind of energy crunch in the early to mid 1960s.

The Beginning of the Commodity Demand Cycle

This energy crunch led to the beginning of the modern commodities investment/demand/supply cycle. Commodities investors continued to enjoy good profits during the period from 1966 to the early 1980s. Gold, corn, oil—it seemed as though all the commodities were in high demand, and investors got rich. There was inadequate supply for the demand of the day.

Then a curious thing happened. As with any business, the drillers, miners, and farmers found it more profitable to engage in their commodities-related businesses. If gold was $120 an ounce and it was profitable to open up a gold mine, how much more profitable would a mining endeavor be if the price of gold were $650 or even $850 an ounce (as it was in 1980)? The same concept was true for oil drillers and people in agribusiness. How much more profitable would a Texas panhandle oil well be if oil was $30 or $40 a barrel as opposed to $12 per barrel in the mid 1970s? What about a basic foodstuff as sugar or corn? Same thing: more profit.

The higher and higher prices from 1966 to 1980 were caused by higher and higher demand. The higher prices also led more people to develop businesses that would extract, mine, drill, or farm for more of the higher profit commodities items. The added mines, wells, and farms added to the supply of the in-demand commodities, and at the same time, technology improved to make more efficient cars, better furnaces for homes, and higher yielding crop seeds. The total effect was a double whammy: more producers and less demand. The net result was falling prices of the commodities in the early 1980s. Gold went from $850 an ounce down to $300 an ounce in a matter of two years. Sugar went to 1/20th of the price it had been ten years earlier. The fuel commodities took a plunge in prices also. In the supply/demand war, the supply side had won. Traders and investors pulled their money out of the commodities markets and prices went down even further.

Commodities Investing Today

The supply glut of the 1980s led investors to look elsewhere to put their money. The late 1990s saw many investors getting into the technology stocks of the day. The returns were so good on tech-heavy indexes that millions of investors poured money into ETFs like QQQ, or the NASDAQ-100 Trust. During these years commodities were flat, some would say even depressed. Kids could go to college hundreds of miles away and still come home every weekend if they wanted, as regular gas was 89 cents a gallon. Someone walking into a high-end jewelry store could buy a one-ounce American Gold Eagle coin for $320 and an American Silver Eagle coin for $5. Supply was high, demand was low, and prices were rock bottom.

Why, you might ask? Everyone was into tech, and they were in it in a big way. Not only was the main street investor putting all of her hard-earned money into high-flying "dot com" stocks, the U.S. dollar was very strong. As an example, Europe's common currency, the euro, was introduced in 1999. It was originally priced to cost $1.17 U.S. dollars for one euro. Things got ugly for the euro soon after its introduction. Since the world's investors wanted to get in on the stock market boom of the time, they were converting massive amounts of euros (and other currencies such as the British pound, also called the pound sterling) into U.S. dollars. This in turn drove the value of the dollar against the euro to higher and higher levels.

This strong U.S. dollar value affected the price of gold in an inverse manner. Since gold is priced in dollars (as well as in euros and British pounds), the price of an ounce of gold fell every time the U.S. dollar got stronger. As the dollar got stronger, more people wanted to hold it as a store of wealth. As the prices of gold and silver fell, fewer and fewer people wanted to hold those metals in their portfolios as a store of wealth. Gold and silver were definitely out of favor.

Soon thereafter, the technology stock boom went bust, and there was a recession. To combat the recession and restore confidence, the U.S. Federal Reserve System—the Fed—lowered interest rates again and again, until the economy was going full steam ahead once more. This time, the developing countries of the world (such as China, India, and Brazil) were on investors' minds as well. These economies were going strong, and their boom brought an increased demand in commodities.

Some of the money that was paid to workers of high-production factories was put into precious metals such as gold and silver. In China, the people's desire for gold had to wait until the government of China gave the go-ahead for gold ownership. Added pressure on the gold market was intense, and the price of gold climbed higher and higher.

The boom of commodities was on: Oil was up to $147 per barrel on July 3, 2008; people were talking about gold going to $1,000, and then $1,250, then $1,500 per ounce as it breached each new level. Other commodities followed suit. The high growth of the world's economies had taken hold, and investors and traders took notice.

Money Supply, Central Banks, Decision Making

Another factor that has led to the rapid rise in the prices of commodities has been the increase in the world's money supply. *Money supply* is a term that is used to gauge the increase or decrease of the electronic and paper money of the world's currencies in relative terms. For example, say there are 1 million $20 bills in circulation (meaning in cash stations, bank vaults, and people's wallets) at the beginning of 2007. In addition to this $20 million in currency, there is an additional $40 million in other denominations of U.S. currency including $1s, $5s, $50s, and $100s. Also, in addition to this paper currency, say there are also $40 million worth of U.S. dollar money in electronic format in bank accounts across the world. With this information, it can be determined that there is $100 million total of the amount of USD (United States dollars) in circulation. This is known as the ***money supply***.

Money supply numbers are calculated by the U.S. Federal Reserve System (*www.federalreserve.gov*) monthly and are reported on its Federal Reserve Statistical Release online at *www.federalreserve.gov/releases/h6/current*. The money supply of the other world currencies are listed on those central bank websites. Since the euro, Japanese yen, and British pound are such major currencies, the quantity of their money supplies are also important.

In the modern world, these countries can modify their money supply a number of ways. Each country's central bank can increase or decrease its own money supply as it sees fit. Most if not all of the time, this is done to regulate either the growth rate of the country's economy or the inflation rate of the country's economy, or sometimes both.

Central banks have many tools at their disposal to help achieve their growth and inflation goals. The most effective way is to change the money supply. If a bank ramps up the money supply of its home currency, it can spur economic growth, or even help a country pull out of a recession. On the other hand, if a country is experiencing growth too rapidly and there is high inflation, the central banks of the country can use tools to decrease the money supply. This decreasing of the money supply will then lead to a cooling of the economy and a lessening of the inflation rate.

Now that you know that a central bank can regulate money supply (and that it is done for a specific reason), you need to know how money supply affects the price of goods, including the price of commodities. Understanding how money supply affects the cost of commodities will help you make a better informed decision on your future commodities investments.

How Money Supply Affects Prices

There is often a change in the prices of goods when the money supply changes. To put it simply, the price of a good will go up when the money supply goes up. In other words, when there are more dollars in circulation, more people hold more dollars (on average) and they have more dollars to pay for the *same amount of goods*. If everyone wanted to buy a loaf of bread, and there were only 100 loaves of bread, then everyone would be pushing and shoving to get their opportunity to buy one of those 100 loaves of bread. In the modern world, they would push and shove with their money. The effect is that each person would try to fight off the other by bidding up the price of the one loaf of bread until the other person couldn't afford it. The price of the bread would go up until it reached a point that people could barely afford. The price would stop at this point. This would be the selling price of the one loaf of bread.

In this example, say that everyone has $100 and the price of a loaf of bread is $10. People could not afford to pay more than $10 for the bread because they had other expenses such as rent, fuel, heat, haircuts, and so on.

If all of a sudden the money supply was doubled, and all of the people in the town now had $200 each, they would be able to spend more on the loaf of bread. This is true because they had more money to spend. Since the number of loaves of bread didn't increase past the original 100 loaves, the bidding war would start up again until the price of the bread reached a new level, and then it would stop, as once again the people couldn't afford to buy it at a higher price. In this example, suppose the price of the bread went to $20 a loaf after the added money supply.

This is an example of inflation through money supply. What happened is that the amount of dollars that people could buy with went up. Each person in the town had double the amount of dollars to spend, but the amount of bread didn't increase.

This is a very simplified example of what has happened and will happen to the world's economies after the banking/housing crisis of 2007–09. The banking and housing crisis beginning in 2007 caused many problems to the world's economy. Many people lost their jobs and their wealth. Unemployment went up to 10 percent in some countries, and the price of valuables such as the stock market fell dramatically. The world fell into a deep recession. In an effort to ward off a depression, the central bankers of the world went on full alert and increased the money supply dramatically. By 2009–10, some economists were saying that the world had seen a four-fold increase in the quantity of money that was in circulation.

Additionally, the central bankers of the world were also lowering interest rates dramatically. This lowering of interest rates allowed commercial banks to lend at lower interest rates, which in turn allowed borrowers to borrow at lower interest rates. This has set the stage for more affordable borrowing and even higher amounts of borrowing, which is the intent and purpose of this action by the central bankers. The combined effect of more money in the system and an easier lending environment is yet to be determined, but one thing is certain: Once the world pulls out of the recession and back to full steam, there will be more people and businesses that have more dollars, euros, and pounds in their pockets. They will be spending this money on things that, for the most part, have not increased in quantity. More money, same amount of things, equals higher prices. Add to this the higher worldwide economic growth and with it more and more consumption of steel, rubber, oil, and other commodities, and there is a strong case for higher commodities prices in the future. A very strong case indeed.

CHAPTER 2

The Basics of Commodities

In this chapter you will learn what makes a commodity. You will also learn a bit about commodity futures, a common yet complex form of trading raw materials. You will also be introduced to other methods of trading and investing in raw materials such as commodities mutual funds and ETFs. You will also be introduced to the concept of investing in companies that mine, grow, or drill for commodities as a business, as this is also a viable investment method.

What Are Commodities?

Commodities are the group of assets that are based upon physical goods. In order to understand this fully, you must understand that other assets such as stocks, bonds, and mutual funds are based upon legal contracts with the companies that they represent.

On the other hand, when you invest in commodities, you are investing in a group of assets that has its value tied to the price of the actual physical thing. In this way, even a paper-based derivative such as a corn future has its upward and downward price movement based on the price of a bushel of actual corn. The same is true for those who trade oil in the spot markets.

FACT

Even though traders are trading on an electronic exchange such as the NYMEX (New York Mercantile Exchange) and using a laptop computer to enter in their trades, what traders are really doing is betting upon the price of actual barrels of light sweet crude oil at the Cushing, Oklahoma, terminal hub.

At the same time, if you would like to add a precious metals portion to your overall investment portfolio, and you go a coin dealer and buy a 50-ounce bar of 0.999+ fine (pure) silver and five 0.900 fine 1918 French 20 Franc Rooster coins (which are 0.1867 ounces of gold each), you are also buying commodities. In this case you are buying the ***actual physical commodity***.

Freely Interchangeable

Another key element to defining a commodity is the fact that each unit of a particular commodity is freely interchangeable with another unit of the same commodity. In this way a fully tradable barrel of North Sea Brent crude oil is considered to be of equal quality and quantity of every other tradable barrel of North Sea Brent crude oil. This is true if the barrel is traded on the Oslo exchange, on the London exchange, or in New York on the NYMEX.

The same standardization of size, quality, and full interchangeability is the hallmark of commodities trading worldwide. A good deliverable 400-ounce bar of 0.995+ fine gold is the same as a good delivery bar of a 400-ounce 0.995+ fine gold bar at any exchange in the world. When you go on an electronic exchange and buy and sell oil, corn, wheat, silver, gold, copper, lead, or cotton, you are buying and selling the rights and ownership of the same quantity and quality of these goods. While the mechanism of the trade might be an electronic (also known as a paper) contract to buy and sell at a later date, the physical good behind the contract is always fully interchangeable.

ALERT

While gold, silver, and copper coins and bars may be of different sizes and quantities, they too can be compared to each other in terms of their composition and weight. This makes one half-ounce gold coin worth very close to the price of every other half-ounce gold coin. The same is true for silver ingots and coins, and copper as well.

On the other hand, if you decide that you would like to accumulate gold, silver, or copper and own the actual physical metal, the coins or bars that you will buy might be of different weights, sizes, or fineness. ***Fineness*** is a term used to identify the purity of the metal in a bar or coin.

Commodities Basics

Commodities are the raw materials of all of the goods that are made and used today. There is not one good or service in the world that does not use commodities in some fashion. A company does not have to be the manufacturer of heavy equipment or other manufactured good to have a need for raw materials in its business. For example, consider the following supply chain showing how a clothing store at the mall depends on commodities:

▼ CLOTHING STORE AT MALL

Potash farmer in Canada harvests fertilizer	oil
Potash farmer ships fertilizer to Georgia cotton farmer	oil
Georgia farmer drives to warehouse to pick up fertilizer	oil
Georgia farmer fertilizes field	oil, potash
Georgia farmer plants cotton seed	oil, cotton
Georgia farmer gathers cotton crop	oil
Clothing manufacturer makes shirts	oil, cotton, and electricity
Store orders finished shirts and has them delivered	oil
Store keeps doors open and sells shirts	oil (heat), electricity (lights, air)

As you can see from the list, commodities are integrated into almost all goods that are sold throughout the world. For example, accountants who work on computers all day use electricity to keep their offices open, lit, and heated, and to operate their computers; they use paper to print out forms and reports, and they buy cheeseburgers and fries for employees who work on Saturday afternoons.

If the company in question were a coffee house, there would be the natural gas in the fireplace, the wheat in the muffin, and the coffee beans in the espresso. If the company were as simple as someone running a newspaper route, there would be the wood pulp in the newspapers, the aluminum in the bicycle, the wool in the fall sweater, and the cocoa in the hot chocolate after the delivery run was over.

Commodities are everywhere and have been used in commerce and development for a very long time. Commodities have represented growth and wealth, and they have been so important to the well-being of communities that great pains have been taken to own, store, and control them. Since commodities are the basic building blocks of what makes the world go around, it makes sense to learn as much as possible about them, including how they can add to your financial well-being through owning and/or trading them. It can be your choice to invest or to trade, with trading looking for short-term gains, and investing going for the long haul. Either way this book will get you up to speed in knowing what direction to take and what commodity and investment method to use that works best for you.

How Commodities Are Traded Today

You can invest in and trade commodities in three ways. The first method is investing and trading through an electronic exchange. Most of these methods involve the buying and selling of standardized contracts in the futures market. This means the contracts represent a freely interchangeable quality and quantity of a commodity. In other words, trading in the futures market is much like trading in units of the commodity.

The Basics of Futures

If you begin to think of the electronic futures exchanges as trading in units of a commodity, you will go a long way in keeping track of the different methods of buying and selling commodities. With the units method, each type of commodity (whether corn, gold, oil, or wheat) is organized into predetermined units. The units may be 1,000 barrels of oil, 5,000 ounces of silver, or 10 metric tons of cocoa. Either way, the number and quality of the commodity is preset. Along with this preset number and quality are other contract specifications such as delivery point.

While it is likely that you will never, ever take delivery of the commodities you are trading in the futures market, the fact is that a commodities contract is what is being traded. In this way, if you were trading gold futures, you would make money on the price estimate of the gold in the contract on the delivery date. Money is made in the change of the price of the gold as it goes up and down (money is made when gold is going down if you are "shorting" gold) when it gets close to the delivery date. At the end, you would make money if the price you are "locked in to buy" at the expiration date of the futures contact was lower than the price of the gold in the open market.

If you want to trade gold, and if you are computer savvy or like the idea of a fast-moving market with high stakes, you could trade the electronic E-micro Gold futures exclusively. E-micro Gold futures allow you to buy and sell contracts of 10 ounces of gold at a time. If you do this you are trading the right to buy one set contract of 10 ounces of gold at a set point in the future. With the E-micro Gold futures, you are trading the right to buy one contract of "good delivery gold" at some point in the future, usually less than three months out.

The concept of trading commodities futures contracts as trading "units" of a commodity is true for all types of futures commodities trading, whether dealing in energy, metals, or agriculture.

Commodity Company Stock, Commodity Mutual Funds

There is a second and undoubtedly easier method for investing in commodities. Buying and selling electronic traded funds (ETFs), stock in commodity companies, and shares in commodity mutual funds are three good ways to gain exposure to the commodity investing arena without the complexity and trouble of futures trading.

With these three methods there is an indirect method of investing. While it is considered "indirect" to invest in a company that mines, quarries, drills, or farms commodities, owning shares of these companies through ETFs, mutual funds, or the stock in the companies themselves can go a long way in allowing you to experience and share in rising commodities prices.

FACT

Think of it this way, if a gold miner such as Barrick Gold Corporation has its mining and refining operations set to be profitable when gold is $1,250 an ounce, they will make $250 profit per ounce when gold is selling at $1,500 per ounce. If gold rises to $2,000 per ounce, Barrack Gold Corporation will still have its operations set to be profitable at $1,250 an ounce, but the company will now earn $750 per ounce in profit, or a 3:1 gain in profitability! This profitability of the company directly tied to the price of the output of the mining operations leads to the value of the stock in the open market. If the stock is priced at $25 when the stock analysts expect gold to be $1,500, the price of the stock will climb in price when gold rises in price. This is because the price of a company's stock is directly tied to its profitability both now and in the future.

If you would like to gain exposure to the commodities world by investing in a commodity company stock, you might also want to consider investing in a commodity mutual fund. ***Commodity mutual funds*** are like other mutual funds in that they allow the shareholder to own part of many different companies at the same time. This allows a diversification process as mutual funds are usually comprised of anywhere from twenty to more than a hundred different company stocks. With this in mind, if you were to buy a commodity mutual fund, you would gain exposure to many different commodity companies at the same time. Some commodity mutual funds diversify further and invest in different commodity areas, including gold, oil, and agriculture all at the same time. In this way these commodity mutual funds are diversified very well, and you as the owner of the commodity mutual fund shares will own part of all of these different companies at the same time. Still other commodity mutual funds invest in derivatives-based ETFs and futures to increase and accentuate the commodity price movement gains. In this way, these funds can offer the best of both worlds and allow you to include both stocks and derivatives into your investment portfolio. (We'll talk more about stocks and derivatives later in this book.)

Commodity Fund Returns

Returns on these commodity mutual funds can be a bit more conservative than returns on a commodity ETF. This is true because the funds usually have most of their money invested in strong, mature, dividend-paying companies. This serves to dampen down the often wild ride that derivatives can provide.

Separate but related to stock investing is investing in commodity ETFs. ETFs are set up like mutual funds in that they are made up of a basket of other financial instruments, like stocks. Unlike mutual funds, which can only be purchased or sold with the end of the day's closing price, ETFs can be purchased at any time during the day. In this way ETFs trade much like a stock, and they can be bought just as easily as a stock through a full-service or discount broker.

ALERT

While many ETFs are set up exactly like a mutual fund in that they are comprised of stocks, some ETFs are set up a bit differently. These ETFs can have their value be based upon a commodities index (much like the S&P 500 Index) and can therefore represent the entire range of commodities investments, including the ones that are not easily traded (like lead and nickel).

If you were to invest in an ETF, you would be capturing the up and down movement of the entire commodities index that it represented. The up and down movement of the ETF would not be based upon a company or group of companies, but rather on the price of the commodities themselves. If used correctly, these commodity index ETFs can be a great addition to an investment portfolio.

Other index ETFs carry the concept further and offer leverage in the commodity position. For example, these leveraged index ETFs will move two times (2x) or three times (3x) the amount of the index, either up or down. This is accomplished with the inclusion of borrowing within the management of the ETF, much like using the power of margin in a stock brokerage account. With this being said, a leveraged 2x or 3x index ETF can move up dramatically when the price of oil, gold, or other commodity swings into play.

This dramatic movement will be especially true with economic announcements coming from any one of the world's largest economies such as China and the United States. If good economic news is to be had from these countries, and that good news means added growth in the future, the commodities indexes will move up also. A commodities index ETF will move up at the same time, while a 2x or 3x index ETF will move up that much more. Leveraged ETFs such as the 2x and 3x ETF can be a good accent to a commodities portfolio. Due to the fact that 2x and 3x index ETFs can have downward movement just as fast, care should be taken with the inclusion of leveraged commodities index ETFs.

Working with Commodity Trading Advisors

In addition to the previously discussed ways in which to invest in commodities, there is also the option of investing with a commodities trading advisor (CTA) and buying private placements/investment partnership shares through your full-service broker. While these methods are not for everyone, they do offer an investor a way to indirectly invest in the commodities market in a passive manner.

You can search for or have your full-service financial advisor recommend a commodities trading advisor. CTAs are licensed to offer advice, make recommendations, and manage clients' money while they invest exclusively in the futures markets. Since the barriers to entry to becoming a CTA are relatively few (all it takes is a test and the financial backing), it is best if you take your time to seek out a reputable CTA much like you would take your time seeking out any other financial professional.

Once you have found a recommended CTA, she can guide you in your commodities futures investments and offer advice as to what to buy, how much to buy, and when to buy. In addition to offering pricing and timing recommendations, CTAs are also licensed to manage your money on your behalf. With this in mind, the CTA will put your money in a futures account and trade it according to your objectives, using the best of her ability.

FACT

If you are thinking of investing with a CTA, take your time, do your research, and ask your other financial advisors if you have them. While investing with a CTA in a professionally managed futures fund may be a way to capture the rapidly moving futures markets, there are some drawbacks.

Having a good CTA working for you can be a very effective way to keep the commodities part of your investment portfolio working to the fullest. This is true because the only job of a CTA is to monitor the commodities futures market and manage commodities futures investments.

One of the biggest drawbacks is the fact that some CTA managed futures accounts require a minimum balance of $25,000 or even $50,000 just to open the account. Other issues include the fact that the advising firm itself is the holder of your money—this means that the financial well-being of the advising firm is critical to the liquidity of your deposits. To put it mildly, if a firm gets into financial trouble, your investment also may be at risk.

Direct and Indirect Investments

There are two final methods for investing in commodities. The first is a very indirect method and the second is a very direct method. With the first, you would gain exposure to the commodities market through the investment and building up of a position in the currencies of commodity-producing nations. The currencies from these commodity-producing nations are called ***commodity currencies***.

The idea is basic. Some countries have very strong natural resources. These natural resources include the mining of gold and silver. The natural resources may also include foodstuffs, wool, and cotton; or they may include coal, iron ore, or copper. Either way, these countries mine and produce natural resources that are then sold in the open market and set for export. In order for other countries to purchase the raw materials of these countries, the buying countries must first put in the order. The buying country then exchanges the home currency for the money of the selling country with the natural resources. This is done in order to pay the bill and take delivery of the commodity. This buying of the commodity-producing country's currency pushes up the price of that currency due to supply and demand.

That said, the price of the commodity currency will rise in value against the other world currencies as the other currencies are buying the commodity currencies in order to pay the bill for the purchased natural resources.

The best way to understand this is through example. Toyota, a Japanese carmaker, wants to buy a shipload of iron ore for its factories. It places an order with Rio Tinto (*www.riotinto.com*) in Sydney, Australia, for one shipload of high-grade iron ore. Before the ship leaves the Sydney, Australia, port, Rio Tinto sends a bill for $1 million Australian dollars to Toyota for the iron ore. Toyota then goes to the Bank of Tokyo and exchanges Japanese yen for Australian dollars by selling Japanese yen in the open market and buying Australian dollars. While this process yields Toyota the money required to pay the iron-ore bill, the selling of yen and buying of Australian dollars has the effect of ever so slightly pushing down the price of the yen while making the price of the Australian dollar go higher. The effect is very, very slight, but when the entire world is doing the same trade with its currency (whether it be Swiss francs, Chinese yuan, U.S. dollars, or Swedish kronor), the effect can be enormous. It can mean that the Australian dollar moves upward 10 percent in a year or even a few months.

That said, it is possible to gain exposure to the commodities market by buying and holding the currencles of the commodity-producing nations, most notably Canada, Norway, New Zealand, and Australia. By owning the currencies of commodity-producing nations you will make money when the economies of these nations strengthen due to increased worldwide demand for raw materials. Buying Canadian dollars, New Zealand dollars, Australian dollars, and Norwegian kroner can add to your portfolio of commodity exposure. How to best go about building a position in these commodity currencies will be discussed later in this book.

The last method of buying raw materials is actually owning them. While it does not make sense to own bushels of corn or bales of cotton, it does make very good sense to own gold and silver coins and bars. This method of owning the physical commodity is best done with gold, silver, copper, and platinum. It can be quite easy and fulfilling to walk into a coin dealer and buy a 10-ounce bar of pure silver. It can also be a sight to hold a pre-1900 European gold coin in your hand and think of the time when that gold was used to purchase goods and pay bills.

In addition to the rare metals of gold, silver, and platinum, you can own and store at your home the industrial metal copper in ingot form. With copper, you can buy the pure form in 1,000-gram bars, or you can even own pre-1982 U.S. 1-cent pennies. Either way, you can choose to go with the most basic form of investing: owning it and holding your investment in your hands. This form of hard-asset investment can be very rewarding and can become a hobby within itself. You can buy coin books and learn the actual gold weights (AGW) and actual silver weights (ASW) in foreign and U.S. coins and hunt for these at flea markets and antique shops in your area. You can also make the trip to your local jewelry store (if they sell gold and silver coins) or buy the gold, silver, or copper coins on the Internet and at auctions such as eBay.

However you decide to invest, you will find there are many ways to get involved and add commodities to your investment portfolio. After reading this book you will learn what might work best for you. All it would take then is for you to go ahead and begin investing in commodities.

CHAPTER 3

Commodities Investing Helps Diversify Portfolios

In this chapter you will learn how commodities are considered an alternative asset class. You will also learn that the returns of an alternative asset class can act to diversify the stocks and bonds in your investment portfolio. The basic concept of what is referred to as an investment cycle will also be covered as well as the basics of up and down commodity price trends. After reading this chapter you will have a good idea of how commodities investing can add to the diversification of your investment portfolio.

Commodities Are an Alternative Asset Class

Any investment advisor will tell you that your goal should be to build an investment portfolio that is not concentrated in one asset. In other words, if you have a portfolio that is invested in only one asset such as one particular stock, the returns of that portfolio will be the ups and downs of only that stock. If you have two or more stocks in your portfolio, your returns will be the weighted average of the returns of the stocks that comprise the entire portfolio. If one stock happens to plummet, another of your stocks may rise, offsetting the reduced returns from the other.

In other words, if you have three stocks in the portfolio, and there is the same dollar amount of each, the returns on the portfolio will be the average of the returns of the three stocks. If one goes down 10 percent and the other two go up 10 percent, you will have an overall return of +3.33 percent.

Stock #1 Down 10% × 1/3 of portfolio = −3.33%

Stock #2 Up 10% × 1/3 of portfolio = +3.33%

Stock #3 Up 10% × 1/3 of portfolio = + 3.33%

Overall return on portfolio of three stocks = +3.33%

Carrying out the idea further, you can see that if you include many stocks (through a mutual fund, for example), you will smooth out the returns of the portfolio even further.

The inclusion of bonds in your investment portfolio would very nearly complete the diversification process and even out the medium- to long-term gains of your portfolio. Bonds alone would not be enough for a totally well-thought-out portfolio. This is because in certain economic cycles (high inflation, growth, uncertainty, etc.), alternative assets such as commodities can outperform even the highest growth stock or the highest yielding bond.

It is best to think of commodities and investing in commodities in the context of the entire investment universe. This term, **entire investment universe**, is meant to conjure up the idea of any and every possible investment vehicle up to and including stocks, bonds, cash, derivatives (such as options), homes, and collectibles such as cars, rare books, and stamps. It consists of everything that can be considered of investment quality and everything that can be considered to belong in an overall investment plan.

ALERT

The idea of not concentrating all of your assets in one asset holds true also with the idea of not concentrating all of your assets in one asset *class*, in this case, stocks. Much like you can smooth out the returns of your investment portfolio with the inclusion of more than one stock, you can smooth out the returns even further with the inclusion of more than one asset class. This can be achieved most simply with the addition of bonds into your portfolio.

With this in mind, you should consider commodities in the class of assets that are called alternative assets. **Alternative assets** are a class of assets that are out of the ordinary grouping of typical assets such as equities (stocks), bonds, or mutual funds.

Alternative Assets

Alternative assets are the grouping of assets that are recommended to be included in an investment portfolio by asset managers who advise high net worth clients. These asset managers are employed at conservative and venerated firms such as Merrill Lynch, Goldman Sachs, UBS, and Credit Suisse. Financial advisors at smaller boutique firms, such as some of the small private Swiss banks, also offer advice on fine and rare art as an investment.

Account holders at these firms are often offered advice as to how to compose their investment portfolios. Most of the time, these firms will recommend that a certain percentage of the overall investment portfolio be invested in alternative assets. The recommended amount can range from 15–20 percent of the overall assets in a client's portfolio.

QUESTION

Why should I buy alternative assets?
Alternative assets are recommended for a portfolio because they usually offer a high level of return that is uncorrelated to the returns that come from traditional assets such as stocks and bonds. A better way to describe "uncorrelated" is when the ups and downs of the alternative asset move independently from the returns of more traditional assets such as stocks and bonds.

Alternative assets are recommended because when assets in other classes such as stocks are falling in value, investment money will flow into high-quality assets of a completely different nature. One example of this is when stocks fall in value, investment grade bonds such as foreign government bonds, U.S. Treasury bills, and notes will rise in value. This rising in value occurs because as the stocks are being sold, the proceeds from the sales are being put into the opposite end of the trade, with one side of the investment trade being the equities or stocks and the opposite being the bonds.

Investment Cycles

An investment cycle is usually considered to last five to seven years. It is expected that during these years, the market's preference for equities and bonds will go back and forth over time. Some months the return of bonds will be higher and some months the return of stocks will be higher.

Since it's impossible to predict the future with 100 percent certainty, most investment advisors will recommend a nearly equal mix of stocks and bonds in an investment portfolio that is set for a five- to seven-year time horizon. This nearly equal mix of equities and bonds will work against each other to create a good chance of conservative, slow, steady gains over the years.

It is true, there are times when both the stock market and the bond market will be performing with low returns, or worse yet, negative returns. In order to combat this it is often recommended that you add 15–20 percent of alternative assets, which would include commodities, to your portfolio mix. This is true because alternative assets such as commodities often-times react independently of the stock and bond market and historically have boomed when the stock market has gone bust. In other words, alternative assets including commodities have returns that are considered to be *uncorrelated to the returns of traditional assets*.

FACT

Alternative assets—including hedge funds, collectibles, art, and commodities—are added to a nearly equal mix of stocks and bonds for further diversification and to smooth out returns despite the natural ups and downs of the market.

Bull and Bear Markets in Commodities

When thinking of how the miscorrelation between alternative assets and traditional assets works, think of a spinning wheel of fortune. As the wheel spins, sometimes stocks will be in the winning zone. As the growth cycle or the time for stocks leaves and everyone has made their money trading stocks, the wind will run out of that class of investments and the investor money will look elsewhere for gains. The market participants will look to put their money into the next thing that will do well for that time: the wheel will take another spin. It might turn up bonds or luxury condominiums or classic cars. It also has a good chance of turning up commodities such as gold, silver, oil, and corn.

A **bear** market fund is one in which, over time, a securities investment (mutual funds, futures, or ETFs) is generally declining. A **bull** market fund is one in which, over time, commodity prices rise over an extended time period, usually when the prices rise faster than they have on a historical basis. In other words, if commodities have risen by 4 percent per year for the past five years and for the past year they have risen by 10 percent or higher, then market analysts would refer to commodities being in a ***bull market***.

The numbers are there to prove this theory. Historically, gold, copper, oil, and other investment-grade commodities will have a bull market when the stock markets and bond markets are in a tug of war and there is little return to be had investing in either.

This function of money flowing to the next best thing is why you need to have a stake in all assets at all times and to consider increasing your position in an asset when it is in play. After the housing bubble burst in the late 2000s, there was a lot of investor money that was looking for a home. Much of it found its way into U.S. Treasury notes and bills, and the prices of these skyrocketed with demand. Much of the money that was not being spent on the collapsed housing market found its way into other physical assets such as precious metals, physical bullion, and ETFs.

FACT

Prices of silver went up from $20 an ounce to $40 an ounce between 2010 and mid 2011, and then fell to around $33 an ounce, staying at this level until the winter of 2011–12. Even the "reduced" price of $33 an ounce for silver bullion represents a return of 65 percent from its starting price of $20 an ounce. The returns of the popular investment-grade gold bullion–backed ETF GLD went from $77 per share to $169 per share from December 2007 to December 2011, a return of nearly 120 percent. On the other hand, the S&P 500 rating went from 1,468 in December 2007 to 1,244 in December 2011, a return of *negative 15 percent!*

Building a well-managed investment portfolio should contain a certain amount of the alternative assets. Most investment advisors recommend that you put 10–20 percent of your overall investments in commodities. With this size investment, you will be able to fully capture gains from any moves in the commodities investment area relative to the returns of the stocks and bonds.

This is true because it is not unheard of that a commodities investment can have returns of 20 percent, 30 percent, or higher during times when commodities are doing well. It may even be that a commodities investment can have returns that far exceed the normal expected returns of the traditional investments such as the stock market and the bond markets.

Core Commodities as Growth Fields

There have been times that the returns of core commodities have doubled in short amounts of time. When crude oil, corn, and gold are in play—meaning when commodities are the hot investment—things can happen quickly. The force of the entire investment community using large amounts of *leverage* (the ability to buy more investments by investing only a smaller amount of actual cash) can push prices very high, very fast. The use of leverage can be equated to the buying of commodities with a credit card, and putting only 5 or 10 percent down, financing the rest. For example, if you wanted to buy $100,000 worth of gold futures, then you would only need to have 5 percent of cash in your futures account, or $5,000. This means that if the gold contract moved up 10 percent, it would now be worth $110,000 or a profit of $10,000. This $10,000 profit would be made on the original $5,000 investment. You can see that the 10 percent movement in gold actually was a 200 percent profit on the original $5,000 investment ($10,000 profit on $5,000.) You can see here that leverage and a fast-moving market can create very high profits indeed!

ALERT

In early 2008, the price of crude oil went from $90 a barrel to around $140 a barrel due to heavy trading by speculators and investors. Gold and silver have had surprising returns as well. During these times the stock market was stumbling and was not offering any confidence to investors.

What causes these movements in price? Sometimes it is demand. Sometimes it is because the asset is in play. Sometimes it is because there is simply too much money in the market and very few good, logical places to put it. It helps to think of it this way: investment money is always there, it is always looking for a home, looking for a place to "land." Luckily for you, it is beginning to be a time in the "spinning of the investment wheel of fortune" in which investment money finds a "home" in hard assets: the commodities.

Since there is a high probability that a commodities investment will yield high returns in the future, a smaller percentage of your investment portfolio needs to be invested in the commodities sector. In this case, a small amount of money will yield big gains when the time comes. That is why financial advisors recommend 10–20 percent of your money be put into gold, oil company stocks, and commodity-based mutual funds. It is only a matter of time until these assets move, and they will move in a big way. In the meantime, there is no need for a huge part of your money to be in the commodities asset class. It would be best if the rest of your money is put in a more stable type of investment such as high-quality stocks and bonds (and cash!).

As you can see, a small amount of investment can be put into your portfolio with the potential to offer big gains. If you have a mix of stocks, bonds, and alternative assets that include commodities, you will have a stable portfolio that has the ability to be financially steady even when traditionally invested portfolios are doing badly. When you have a percentage of money in gold, oil, copper, corn, etc., you will be able to gain when other things such as stocks or bonds are going down in value. The idea is that a well-thought-out commodities investment plan will add to the overall return of your investment when other assets aren't doing so well.

Thus, no investment portfolio is complete without the addition of a certain percentage of commodities in the overall portfolio. This is because of the uncorrelated returns aspect of commodities investments relative to traditional assets such as stocks and bonds.

One of the best ways to include alternative assets in your portfolio is the investment in commodities. There are many ways in which to do this:

through futures, commodity company stocks, commodity-based mutual funds, ETFs, or the actual commodities themselves (such as owning actual gold coins, silver bars, or copper bullion.)

Risk and Reward

Now that you know some of the fundamentals and principals of diversification, you can make a better informed decision as to the appropriateness of commodities in your investment portfolio. Since one of the core ideas to diversifying a portfolio is to increase the potential for returns while minimizing the overall risk of the portfolio, it makes sense to consider the risk of commodity assets as a group.

There are many ways of investing in commodities, some riskier than others. There is a range of investing risk that goes from highly leveraged futures investments to more stable, indirect investing such as putting money in a commodity company stock or even a commodity stocks mutual fund. With this in mind, you can choose to build your exposure to the commodities world in such a way that there is a great amount of risk (and reward), or you can choose to build your investments in commodities to be lower risk (and lower reward) if that matches your investor risk/return profile.

QUESTION

What can I expect in terms of gains?
What are some of the gains that can be expected with an investment in commodities? Depending on the type of investment vehicle, your returns could range from 100 percent annually or higher with derivatives such as futures (which carry added risk) to 5–15 percent annually if you were to invest in a conservative stock mutual fund, which carries less risk.

As you go through this book, you should begin to think of your individual risk/return profile. You may be a low-risk type of person who has a very conservative investment portfolio that is invested mostly in bonds. If this is the case, you may consider yourself very risk adverse. On the other hand, if you are the type of person who has a greater percentage of your portfolio in high-growth stocks, you would most likely be considered to be more risk accepting.

Keep thinking of what type of investor you are when you read this book. In addition, try to get an idea as to what type of returns you would like to make from your investment in commodities. Also, try to think of what goals you have for investing in commodities. These goals can be very individualized in nature. They can range from increasing the stability of your overall investment portfolio, to greatly increasing the return of a conservative bond portfolio by investing in a commodity futures pool, to owning what some people consider the ultimate safe haven investments: gold and silver.

CHAPTER 4

Sourcing Information for Fundamental Analysis

Fundamental analysis is the predicting of price movements with the help of financial and economic data and is one of the keys to determining what commodity to invest in and when to invest in it. Learning how to perform fundamental analysis isn't that hard. Having access to up-to-date information, knowing where to look for data, and building up your own online info presence are some of the topics covered in this chapter.

What Is Fundamental Information and Analysis?

When you are beginning to trade and invest in commodities, what you should be looking at is whether it is a good time to invest and at what price should you invest. One of the best ways to determine these variables is to use information wisely, which starts with knowing where to get the information that you will use in your study of commodities and the economics of commodities.

The study of the economics of investments can be called fundamental analysis, or reading the fundamentals. ***Fundamental analysis*** is the study of the big picture of an investment within the economies of an investment sector (such as raw materials) or a country (such as China) or an economic area (such as Europe). When someone says they are studying the fundamentals of an investment, what they are saying is that they are studying the investment by looking at the cash flows of a country, the growth of product development within a growing country, or even the economy of a country or the world as a whole.

The fundamental analysis of commodities investing is the study of individual companies, countries, and the world's consumption of the world's raw materials. If you are studying the fundamentals of a possible investment in gold, you may consider the following facts:

▼ **GOLD**

What	Where	Implication
Increased money supply	Central bank websites	Inflationary pressures
Increased jewelry demand	Gold industry websites	Increased price pressure
Central bank buying/selling	Bank for International Settlements/ International Monetary Fund websites	Up/down price of gold
Foreign holiday seasonal demand	Gold industry news websites/ Historical trends	Timing of upward price pressure

Since fundamental analysis involves reading and studying the bigger picture, you will also need to have a time frame of a bigger picture, usually two to three months on the short side and up to five to seven years on the long side. To contrast, some traders look at the very short and ultra-short time frames, which would include predicting the price of a commodity in the next day or two, or even the next hour or two. Even if you are looking to shorten your time horizon and look at the two-day/two-hour time frame, it would be best if you have a good idea of the fundamentals of the commodity you are trading, as this will give you a good view as to the overall direction of that commodity, whether it be up or down.

ALERT

It is best to consider all of the facts before you put your money into an investment. The same holds true for investing and trading in raw materials. Getting a firm grasp on the overall present and future demands of commodities will go a long way in allowing you to be confident in the choice of which commodity to invest in and the timing of that investment.

Sourcing Financial Information

In order to get the most out of your investments you will need to learn what to look at with fundamental analysis and where to find the information. The best places to find fundamental, or "big picture," information is at the public and private level, which includes both paid-for reports and free access corporate websites and central banking websites.

Since you are looking for ideas as to what type of raw material to invest in, it would be best if you start by looking at the different types of commodities that make up some of the better known commodities indexes. These commodities indexes are financially engineered baskets of common raw materials. The indexes are set up just like the Dow 30 or the S&P 500, in which they record the average price weighting of individual components. (The Dow 30 consists of the thirty largest and most widely-held public companies in the Dow Jones Industrial Average.) The Dow Jones–UBS

Commodity Index (*www.djindexes.com/commodity*) is comprised of the prices of the following raw materials:

▼ COMMODITY CLASS	COMMODITIES	SAMPLE INDEX RATING IN %
Energy	Natural Gas, Oil, Heating Oil, Unleaded Gasoline	33.90% of the entire index*
Agriculture	Corn, Soybeans, Wheat, Soybean Oil, Sugar, Coffee, Cotton	28.79%
Precious Metals	Gold, Silver, Platinum	16.07%
Industrial Metals	Copper, Aluminum, Zinc, Nickel	14.92%
Livestock	Live Cattle, Lean Hogs	6.32%

*Indicates the percentage of the commodity class in the index

Commodities indexes such as this one use the basket approach to calculate the average price movement of basic raw materials in general. In the basket method, the index will take a base price of each of the commodities set with a historical price level. This date in the past will be the same for all of the raw materials in the index. After the prices are found at the historical date, the trading price of each of the commodities in the basket will be set to 100 and weighted according to the basket percentage to get the current index rating relative to the original base year that is set at 100.

FACT

As time moves on and the prices of commodities move up and down, the base price of 100 in commodities indexes will be adjusted.

This means that if copper had a base year of 1990 and a trading price of $1 a pound, and now copper trades with a price of $3.75 per pound, the base index price of copper will have gone from 100 to 375. The same is true for all of the individual components of a commodities index. If oil goes up, its base index will go up, even if on the same day another commodity such as lean hogs goes down. As the day is recorded (or moment to moment recorded with a tradable index such as the UBS mentioned here), some commodities will be going up while others will be going down. The commodities index will then take the base index movement multiplied by the weighing in percentage terms of that commodity. In other words, if the index has livestock set at 5 percent of the index, and livestock moves up 2 percent then the index will "weight" the 2 percent gain of the livestock to only 5 percent of the total index (2 percent $\times$ 5 percent = adding 0.1 percent of the total index for the day.) The resultant numbers of all commodities will be added up, and what is left is the upward or downward percentage movement of the entire commodities index, which has taken into account the up and down movement of the entire commodities investment universe. With this in mind, you can dissect the basic component from the list to come up with the elements—energy, agriculture, precious metals, industrial metals, and livestock—in their percentage terms; in other words, how the movement of one particular commodity compares with the movement of the entire commodities investment universe. Or, you can watch how particular commodities move independently by using a simple futures monitoring program such as Yahoo! Finance or the Google Finance Watch List. If you use these programs, you can enter in each element of the index basket as its own symbol, and then enter in the appropriate weighting in percentage terms.

Building an Online Financial Presence

Using the method of building online finance websites to track the prices of commodities and commodities indexes can be a really fun and easy way to keep track of how the commodities markets are doing from each trading day to the next. You can also use the Google Finance "Portfolios" section (*www.google.com/finance*) to build two or three portfolios: The first one or two can use the weightings of the one or two well-known commodities indexes, while the third can be used to keep track of the buy and sell ratings from your full-service broker.

FACT

Remember, you are looking for information at this point. Sometimes, the best way to get information is to just begin to poke around websites and build imaginary portfolios. Some professional commodities traders run simulated portfolios at the most basic level.

While it is possible to open a demo, or practice trading account, at a commodity trading firm in order to try out new ideas, you may find it much easier to test drive a new commodity advisor or information website by entering in the trades that they recommend at the percentages that are recommended. In this way, you can test out the quality of the advice you are receiving even if you are not set up or even thinking about buying commodities futures, ETFs, or funds. In this way, you will use Google Finance (*www.google.com/finance*) or Yahoo! Finance (*http://finance.yahoo.com*) as a monitoring tool. This monitoring can also be known as a simplified form of "price discovery." **Price discovery** is the process of knowing how much your goods (gold coins, silver bars, gold, silver, or copper scrap) or securities (mutual funds, futures, or ETFs) are worth both at the buying point and at the present.

One of the key elements in building up a skill in trading or buying commodities is getting a feel for the price of the commodity. If you haven't looked at the price of silver in three months and you are in a coin shop to buy an average-quality 1921 U.S. Peace Silver dollar (which is 0.900 fine, or 90 percent pure silver), how can you expect to know what is a good price? If you haven't been monitoring the price of a well-known commodities index, how will you know when is a good time to get into your favorite commodities mutual fund? If you haven't seen that copper has gone from $3.25 a pound to $4.15 a pound in the past nine months, how will you know that it may be time to start sorting U.S. pennies, or to buy into that copper mining stock that your broker keeps recommending? Information is key to getting to know the market. Getting to know the market begins with building and setting up mock portfolios in Google Finance or Yahoo! Finance.

Full-Service Brokers

A full-service commodities broker or financial advisor such as Credit Suisse or Merrill Lynch can offer advice as to the prevailing market conditions for sub-groups of commodities. If you are so inclined, you can subscribe to some of the newsletters that are published by some of the oldest money-management firms in the world: the private Swiss bankers. One example is UBS, which is a full-service firm with headquarters in Zurich, Switzerland (*www.ubs.com*). Any one of these firms or your commodity trading advisor can offer you up-to-the-week market reports on the supply and demand of the raw materials that you trade and invest in. Many of these reports, called ***brokers' reports***, also offer advice as to timeline for investment, which includes when to get into and out of a trade successfully and profitably.

These brokers' reports can be a key element to the success of your investing in raw materials. This is true because the full-service brokers and commodities trading advisors employ highly educated and experienced staff to analyze and predict the best commodities to get into and at what price. What is more, the people who write the reports and the investment firms that publish the reports have a vested interest in your success. They know that if you give them a chance and look at the advice they give in their brokers' reports, they have a good chance of turning you into a full-time client.

Being a Savvy Customer

This brings up a very important element in the process of gathering information about your potential investments in general, and raw materials specifically. One of the key elements in managing your money, building up assets, and making decisions about what to invest in is knowing what to look for and then knowing who to trust. It seems as though many people are very eager to trust mutual-fund companies and no-name discount brokers, but these same people have a slight distrust of the people who give advice and reports, provide the investing ideas, and sell the actual gold, silver, and platinum coins and bars that are the basics of commodities investing.

It is best not to find yourself in this trap: It is better to keep in mind that commodities trading advisors; discount futures brokers such as Apex-Futures (*www.apexfutures.com/trading-platforms/apextrader*); full-service firms such as Credit Suisse (*https://www.credit-suisse.com*), Northern Trust Corporation (*www.northerntrust.com*), and UBS (*www.ubs.com*); and precious metals dealers such as the Chicago-based Harlan J. Berk, Ltd. (*www.harlanjberk.com*) are in the business of providing their clients with the best investing advice and tools. Whether it be placing a trade on an online platform, putting in a large investment in a commodity-based fund, or buying a brand-new sealed tube of 0.999 pure Austrian Philharmonic silver coins at your local coin dealer, it is best to develop an idea that most firms are in the business of getting and then keeping customers.

With this in mind, your full-service broker knows it should try very hard to give the best information to its clients. If UBS feels as though gold is a strong buy, because the firm's analysts have a solid feeling that gold will go up another 12–15 percent in the next twelve months, and they know that the world's traders are pushing down the price of gold due to a rise in the value of the stock market, these highly trained analysts will still issue a "strong buy" order on gold (or coffee, copper, or any other commodity). These analysts know they are operating in the best interests of their clients, and that their clients' successes in investing are directly correlated to their success. A happy, profitable, successful investor will stay and likely will be a client for life.

The same is true for an online discount futures dealer. The owners of the firm know you are counting on them for quality information and execution. They know you will not be a customer for long if there is any perceived problem with their company or service.

ESSENTIAL

There is also a vested interest in a coin dealer or jewelry store that sells precious metals over the counter. These dealers can be very small and private, and their clients' choice to deal with them can be highly personal: either you like the dealer or you don't. These dealers are in business too, and they count on repeat business and word of mouth to be successful.

Keep this idea in mind when you begin the process of investigating different sources of information and eventually decide which online futures firm, CTA, full-service firm, or coin dealer you will be using to buy and accumulate your position in raw materials and commodities.

Other Ways to Get Information

In addition to getting privately published information known as brokers' reports, you can source out information that is available over public Internet sites and at newsstands and bookstores. Financial news websites such as the *Wall Street Journal*'s MarketWatch (*www.marketwatch.com*) and Seeking Alpha (*http://seekingalpha.com*) offer free high-quality information regarding all aspects of investing and trading.

Some information news sites offer more general base information. Reading these sites can provide an introductory level of information and serve to get you up to speed as to what the market is saying about the commodities end of the investment spectrum. In addition to these sites, cable stations such as CNBC and Bloomberg can offer readings as to the "pulse" of the market, as there are frequent individual reports on the prices of gold, oil, copper, and other frequently traded commodities.

CHAPTER 5

Fundamental and Technical Analysis

Once you have the basic idea that you would like to begin investing in commodities, you will need to know which commodity to invest in and at what price. More details as to the timing of your commodity investing and trading can be found by performing the two different types of analysis and then comparing the results. These two types of analysis are called (1) economic, or fundamental, analysis and (2) charting, also called technical analysis.

Sources of Fundamental and Technical Data

Knowing when is the best time to get into trading and investing in commodities can make the difference between profits or loss. Instead of accumulating assets without knowing where the price of the assets has been and will go in the future, it is better to do some economic, or fundamental, analysis on the subject of past demand and future demands for raw materials before your first trade is made. This **fundamental analysis** of past and future demands is done by studying central banking websites and economic data.

On the other hand, **technical analysis** is the study of mathematical trends that appear on trading charts. Whereas you study central banking websites and economic data for fundamental analysis, you would use graphic charts of past prices to sketch data points to arrive at a prediction of future prices of the commodity.

While there is much to be discovered from each type of analysis, when you combine the two of them in one study, the results can be quite a powerful trading system.

ESSENTIAL

Financial and trading analysis is divided into two categories: fundamental analysis and technical analysis. *Fundamental analysis* is the study of the "soft" information: economic growth, money supplies, inflation figures, etc., while *technical analysis* is the study of "hard" information: mathematics, ratios, and how they relate to opening and closing prices.

The key to using this dual system is to build a platform in which you have evidence of which commodity to buy (and sell) and when. So, although the ideas presented in this book will give you the big picture and argument for trading commodities, the fact is that you will need to supplement this information in order to develop enough knowledge to know when is a good *time* to begin a program of accumulation of commodities.

In essence, this book will serve as a launching board for your knowledge: it will serve as the basic argument that an investment in raw materials and trading commodities is good. Next, you need to do some research as to when will be the best time to buy these commodities, and to know what types of commodities are set to move in price. This goal can be best achieved by a multilayered and multipronged disciplined study of written and televised information, supplemented with chart analysis.

This information can come from a disciplined reading program and frequent visits to websites that offer well-thought-out and well-educated analysis. To obtain this you could be visiting websites of the *New York Times*, *Wall Street Journal*, and the *Economist*. In addition to these sites, you should make it a habit to visit the sites of the central banks of the countries with an emphasis on the larger economies. This would include the central banks of Europe, Sweden, Japan, the United States, and of course the commodity-producing countries of Australia, New Zealand, Canada, and Norway. Other recommended readings would include some of the better business magazines, as well as articles that appear on CNBC's free iPad website, and of course the cable version of live CNBC and Bloomberg. Your goal for studying these sources of information includes looking for any hint of growth, the supply and demand of commodities, growing money supplies, quantitative easing, and lowering interest rates—basically, the type of macroeconomic information that can support the idea that commodities will be going into high demand and therefore high prices.

Technical Analysis in General

You will need a focused source of information for your technical analysis data. For most, this information will come from their full-service brokers in already-analyzed form with buy and sell price recommendations. For others, this information will have to be "built" from charts that can be drawn on their online brokerage accounts. Most futures brokers have built-in software that allows beginning clients to access some of the basic charts such as bar charts and candlestick charts (see discussion of candlestick charts later in this chapter). These charts can be easy to call up with the click of a mouse; from there the analysis can be done with the trading account's trading software.

Some of the best ways to assimilate technical information are to draw the charts using the software and combine your recommendations with the thoughts and recommendations of your full-service broker. The key ingredient in technical analysis is to use several types of analysis and to cross-check your findings against the findings you have determined from fundamental analysis.

FACT

Most online trading platforms are adaptable to be programmed to show technical indicators. If your trading platform allows this, it is best to take the broker's online tutorial to help you get established with your knowledge of how the software works. Once you have a handle on how to make charts, you're off and running!

The key places to look for information are the world's central banking websites. As mentioned before, the best way to look at the sites is to search for signs of growth. This growth might be shown by an increase in a country's actual or estimated growth rate as measured in an increase in its gross national product.

Also look for a raise in the interest rates of the country's currency, as this would signal a heating up in that nation's economy, and the increase in the interest rate would signal efforts to slow the economy in the home country.

Other issues to look for would be hard data on inflation. If there is a set inflation figure of the economic managing body of the country, it will be shown in that central bank website. Look for a target inflation rate stated on the website in the charter of that central bank. Very near this information will be the actual inflation rate of the nation. These inflation figures are usually held in a tight rein, and if there is any amount that exceeds the inflation rate, the central bank will be quick to act to reduce the inflation. This actually happened in the United States in the early 1980s when inflation was running high due to a combination of tax incentives, high commodity prices, and higher and higher wages. As a result, the Federal Reserve hiked interest rates as high as 18 percent to curb the strong inflation, which in turn, had the effect of slowing the economy to a recession level, effectively putting the brakes on the inflation rate.

While this is one of the hard facts of banking, the economies of recent years have included factors that may include a lessening of the rein on inflation. This is due mainly to the banking and housing crisis of 2007–09. These crises led to a special circumstance for central banks, and the largest countries have generally agreed upon loosening the rein of inflation as the best remedy for the ills of the world's economies.

More on Fundamental Data Sources

Commodity company and commodity industry websites can also be good sources of information about the direction of the demand for raw materials. You might have the notion that the information on commodities company websites would be biased. It is true that while the facts will be presented in the best light, they will be facts, as these companies are regulated by the Securities and Exchange Commission (SEC) in the United States and its equivalent in other countries.

Knowing this means that you can also use company website data to confirm your ideas about when is a good time to buy commodities. Since the companies that mine, drill, or grow raw materials have a vested interest in attracting and retaining shareholders, they will offer insights into the economy, the commodities industry, and their specific commodity as a whole.

This also means that these firms will have hard data that you can cross-reference against the data found on the industrial websites, such as association sites that end in ".org." These sites are more research based and also offer a chance to see into the commodities business from a producer and consumer point of view.

One of the best examples of these ".org" websites is the World Gold Council (*www.gold.org*). This site offers information about the past, present, and future demand of gold as it equates to jewelry manufacturing demand, investment demand, and bank holdings. It also offers insight into the planned central bank buying and selling, and how this will ultimately affect the price of gold in the short and long term. This is one of the better websites about gold-investing information.

Other sites include Kitco Metals (*www.kitco.com*), the *Oil & Gas Journal*, (*www.ogj.com/index.html*) as well as the U.S. Department of Energy (*http://energy.gov*) and the U.S. Department of Agriculture (*www.usda.gov*).

Other sources of information can come from your full-service broker's websites as well as from some of the public access portions of some of the world's private bank websites. These private banks are often located in Europe in general, and in tax havens specifically. A list of all of the Swiss banks can be found at SW Consulting SA's website, (*www.swconsult.ch/cgi-bin/banklist.pl*); this site is one of the best listings on the Internet of private banks. In addition to the names, Swiss banks by Canton, and addresses, there is a live hyperlink to each bank's website.

QUESTION

Where else can I get information for fundamental analysis?
You can find some of the best sources of information for fundamental analysis by going outside of your regular broker's websites. Try researching the competing trading houses such as Goldman Sachs, Merrill Lynch, and Morgan Stanley's home websites to see what information they are offering about commodities trading.

Knowing about commodities trading and investing goes hand in hand with knowing about banking and about the world economy. Since this is true, you will learn a lot of these subjects by spending a Friday evening in front of the TV with iPad or laptop in hand. Take your time going through the lists of banks. You may have to select "English" from the other languages available (mainly French and German.) You will notice that most of the sites will offer guidance as to where they believe the market will be in the near and medium term. Most of the private banks will have a commodities trading desk or will offer investors a commodities product, such as a managed account, much like a hedge fund or managed futures fund. If the bank offers these products, you are in luck! Read any information they are offering. After a few nights of reading the sites (it will take you some time to work your way through the entire list of Swiss banks as there are hundreds), you may notice evidence that many of the money managers at these banks are thinking the same thing: it is time to buy commodities! They may each have different target prices and different entry and exit points. But if they are, in general, setting the stage for investors to look toward the future with their investments, then you have further evidence that it is time to begin your investment and trading process of acquiring commodities and commodities-based assets. Remember, you are looking for sources of information that show growth, money supply, inflation, and commodities demand. These will be your sources of information for your fundamental analysis. In essence, you are looking for evidence to well-thought-out arguments that it is the right time to accumulate commodities.

Basic Technical Indicators

After looking at your sources for key information and evidence that it is a good time to buy into commodities, you should then look for technical evidence as to what is the best entry point and exit point in which to buy and sell the commodity.

This technical information includes the use of statistics, mathematics, charts, and regression analysis to quantitatively determine the optimal entry and exit point of trades. While fundamental analysis is information and evidence for the medium and longer term direction of the metals, energies, and grains, technical analysis is for shorter term, usually a week or less.

The basic theory of technical analysis is that a trader would be able to time her trade by looking at the charts alone. She would be able to look at a bar chart and use the software on her trading platform to draw lines that are statistically significant. With this data she would then mark the point to buy and sell. This drawing of lines can be done quite easily, but knowing how to interpret them can take a bit of training.

FACT

Data can be drawn from basic elements. These basic elements include candlestick charts, regression analysis, and resistant and support levels. Some of the more complex methods include Elliott wave principle and moving averages. Remember that you are looking for information to augment your fundamental analysis and using the combination of these methods to make educated decisions as to when and what to buy.

Once you have the fundamental analysis done and you have concluded that there is a commodity that you would like to trade, such as copper (which would have to be traded in a futures account), you would then go the trading platform and call up a basic chart such as a line chart.

A line chart is composed of the copper futures' movement for each of the trading periods. Once you have the chart on your screen (and you can find it by clicking on "line chart" on your trading platform), the next thing you need to do is to set a time frame. You will have the choice of short time frames such as one minute, and longer time frames such as one hour and one day. Choose one that is in between, such as a fifteen-minute chart. This will be a good place to start, but after you get the chart started, you will be able to switch among all time frames with ease.

After you have called up your basic line chart and switched it to a medium time frame, you should then go to the part of your software that allows you to choose different types of technical indicators. From this point you can choose "Add Technical Indicators," and then you can choose "50-Day Moving Average." At this time you should also select "200-Day Moving Average."

These two moving averages, the 50-day and the 200-day, are mathematically figured to average the prices of the copper futures over those time frames. These are the key buy and sell indicators for those who are traders. The combination of the two will show where the price of the copper futures (or any other tradable and therefore chartable asset such as an ETF or mutual fund) will change direction. The theory is simple; look for where the 50-day and the 200-day moving averages cross: at this point the price will change either up or down.

Once you have these points on your chart, you know when to set your buy and sell points. If you are buying electronic commodities such as futures or ETFs, you can set your trading software to automatically buy a set number of shares when this price is reached. If you are buying and accumulating physical gold and silver coins and bars, then you can use this as a timing guide as to when to go to your coin dealer to buy more of the precious metals (or to buy online).

Support and Resistance Levels as Indicators

Support and resistance indicators can also give trading information. These indicators will show the point at which the commodity will have a ceiling and a floor in price. This means that the commodity will rise or fall in price between these two price levels. The prices will generally move up and down between the two as if caught like a bouncing ball. With the graphic representation of a support and resistance level, you can visually see when a commodities price will begin to slow and then reverse in price.

The action of the price will be simple. It will move up closer and closer to the resistance point and then stop and pause. At this time the other traders around the world who are watching the price of the commodity will also see the slowing and stopping of the price movement. They will then issue "sell orders" and begin to slowly dismantle their positions and lock in the profits they have at that point. Since all of the traders out there will be looking at the same information, they will all be looking at the same support and resistance lines. The net effect of many traders looking at the same resistance line on their computers and then issuing sell orders leads to heavy selling pressure worldwide. This selling pressure usually leads to a lowering of prices and a backing off of the price of the commodity from the resistance points.

Once the selling pressure has reduced the price of the commodity to a low enough level, the market participants will begin bidding up the price of the commodity again. Bid by bid, the price of the commodity will rise until it reaches the resistance point once again. When this happens the movement of the price will slow and stall, and once again the world's traders will begin a selling campaign, taking their profits off the table. The process will repeat itself over and over again until the resistance point is breeched and passed through. Once this new price level is held over for a few days, this will become the new price resistance point. Sometimes there will be enough momentum to carry the price of the commodity to a point that is quite a bit higher. When this happens there will be much activity in the market, and the price of the commodity will seem to soar above the previous holding point of the resistance level. This can cause quite a stir in the market and oftentimes will be hotly talked about on CNBC and Bloomberg TV.

ESSENTIAL

When a commodity is getting near a statistically and psychologically important resistance level, the world's market commentaries will often predict what level the commodity might go to once the resistance level is breeched and passed through. This is what consists of most of CNBC's airtime: market experts predicting resistance-level breeches and the next "breakout" level.

This is because a break in price past the resistance level is considered very significant and psychologically important. It will sometimes seem as though the market has gone wild, and rightly so! There is often a surge in trading with higher and higher prices as the public takes notice that the commodity is in play. The price of the commodity will go directly to the next resistance point before selling off again to a halfway point between the lower and higher resistance levels.

The resistance level process works the same for support levels (floor prices, or low price points), but in reverse. The support price will be "tested" on the way down again and again if the prices are falling. Once a support level is breached, the price will fall quickly to the next support level. At this point, the traders in the market will begin buying again, and the buying pressure will drive the price up to a level above the old support level but below the higher support level (which is now the first resistance level).

Candlestick Charts and Volume Indicators

Drawing a support and resistance level for a commodity can be just as easy as drawing any of the other technical indicators on your bar chart. In order to do this, first draw a bar chart, and then go to the part of your trading software that allows you to call up and draw these indicators. There are many types of technical indicators that you can use to determine what are good buy and sell points. While they are all useful, it would be good to get familiar with the basics: support levels, resistance levels, and moving averages.

There are two other indicators and charts that can be used to gather trading information. The first is called the **candlestick chart** or Chinese lantern chart. It is easy to switch between a bar chart and a candlestick chart with your trading software. A candlestick chart is different from a bar chart in that it not only shows the range of the commodity price during that period (one minute, fifteen minutes, thirty minutes, one hour, etc.), it will also show the opening price and the closing price of the period. The opening price will be shown by a small "tail" to the left side of the price bar, and the closing price will be shown by a small "tail" to the right side of the bar. In addition to this information, different colors of the bars will indicate a higher price than that in the last time period, and a different color for a lower price than that of the previous time period. This information can be useful in determining the overall price movement of the commodity over time.

The other indicator is a **volume indicator**. You can choose to have your trading software show the trading volume for each time period. By selecting this function, you will be able to see whether a price spike or valley is accompanied by heavy volume. Volume that has been building at a price that is close to a resistance point could mean a break past that price point. This could indicate a good time to "go long" in that commodity meaning it is time to add to your position soon! *Going long* refers to a trade that will make money when the market goes up. Going long is a trading term for buying, as opposed to going short, which means selling (a contract, ETF, stock, etc.)

CHAPTER 6

Looking for Setups

Once you have read the fundamental and technical information and have concluded that it is a good time to buy commodities, you can then get into the phase of trading that is called "looking for setups." A *setup* is when conditions are right to create the best time to buy or sell your commodity; that is, you can get into a particular trade with a good chance of making a profit. Looking for setups can be the fun part of trading. It is the time of waiting for the perfect moment.

Read the News, Read the Charts

Getting the right information is the first step in learning to know when and what to trade. In Chapter 5, you learned some of the basic forms of fundamental and technical analysis tools. Once you get familiar with reading central banking websites and brokers' reports and studying industry websites, you will get a "big picture idea" of commodities trading.

You should build up knowledge of the fundamentals that go behind the raw materials' industry and demand. Most of the time the information will overlap. Brokers' reports, magazine articles, and TV shows will be offering the same information about the economy, money supply, and inflation.

Once you have this information, you will be faced with the task of turning it into knowledge of the business of buying and selling commodities. It takes a knack for reading facts, watching news on TV, feeling the pulse of the market, and then turning these observations into a plan of action. This plan of action would start with an actual written, workable plan to build a position in gold or silver bars, a portfolio of commodities ETFs, or to build up shares in a commodities mutual fund.

In addition to building up knowledge of the commodities market from your study of the fundamental indicators, you can add your study of technical indicators. Some say that money can be made on trading anything by looking at the charts alone (technical analysis). These people believe and trust in the math behind the trades. They believe in a crowd psychology, ratios, and statistics. These same people think nothing of the other side of the equation. They think nothing of central bankers' speeches, a hike in interest rates, an increase in money supply, or an increase in the gross national product of an economic zone. Pure technical analysts think only of the data on the charts. Studies have proven that this technique can offer very effective insight into the potential direction of a commodity (or other traceable product, such as a commodity ETF).

Even more studies have shown that the combination of the study of fundamental information and the study of technical information will lead to the strongest trading system. This is true because the information will form a "cross hatch" and will build itself, offering confirmation of your buying signals again and again.

ALERT

Remember, you will be looking for signals of what to buy, when, and at what price. More precisely, you will be looking for evidence that the economy is heating up, which would cause the supply of commodities to go down and thus demand of commodities (and therefore prices) to go up.

Work to develop a system of cross-checking the evidence of buying and selling signals from your "soft information," or your fundamental analysis, with the evidence from your "hard information," or your technical analysis. You will find that the combination of these two will lead to the strongest buy and sell signals, and will give you the clearest indication of the direction of the commodity you are trading.

Sit Tight, Wait for the Trough

The key element in doing fundamental and technical analysis is knowing when it is *about to be the best time to trade.* Once you have done both analyses and determined that it is just about the best time to invest, you should sit and wait for the trough. In this manner, you will be adding an extra layer of safety to your buying program.

Waiting for the trough is the same thing as "buying on the dips" with the added notion of waiting for a slowing of the momentum of the commodity's price movement. Oftentimes a commodity will be at the point that suggests a buying opportunity. Since most of the world's traders in that commodity will be looking at the same information on their screens, there will be the same reaction across the investing community.

The reaction is that there will be a pause in buying (or selling). This process will be very evident when looking at the charts. It will seem as though time is ticking by with very little movement in the price of the commodity. But after this pause, the price will move up again.

How long will the pause last? The neat part is that the pause will always be in proportion to your buying timeline. This means that if you are day trading commodities futures, the pause will still be noticeable, even if it is ultra-short term of only thirty seconds to one minute.

On the other hand, if you have a plan to slowly build up a position in a specific commodity over several seasons or a year, the pauses will still come. In these cases, the pause might be over a weekend or before a trading holiday. In any case, the pause will be a long enough time to notice it and, if you are so inclined, to do a bit of buying!

ESSENTIAL

While you are waiting for the trough, take the opportunity to build up a position in cash. If your financial advisor recommends a certain percentage of your account in cash, think of increasing this amount. This cash stash will also act as "dry powder" to be readily available when buying opportunities come up.

The best thing to do is to get your research early by staying abreast of the fundamentals. Go over the fundamentals on a continuous basis. Keep the flow of reading, studying, and watching the news and websites in your routine. Next, log into your trading platform when you can and draw up some charts. After you have determined that good times to buy are approaching, sit and wait for the perfect opportunity. If you are short term, set up the software to get ready to make a trade. This system would work as if you were day trading a commodity. If you are longer term, you set aside money in your account to buy the number of ETFs, mutual fund shares, or physical metal when the time comes.

With a bit of training and patience, you can learn to gently buy (or sell) the commodity and almost scoop up your position just before the price begins to move.

The U.S. Dollar and Commodity Pricing

There is an inverse relationship between the price of some commodities and the value of the U.S. dollar. This is true for gold, silver, and oil. The main reason for this is that these commodities are sold all over the world priced in U.S. dollars. With this comes the fact that as the price of the dollar falls relative to other currencies of the world, the price of a barrel of oil or an ounce of gold will go up in price. This process acts as a seesaw effect: the purchasing power of the dollar goes up and down against the fixed value of the commodity.

Keep in mind that the value of the purchasing power of the dollar is one-half of the equation in the daily price of gold, silver, and oil. The other half of the trading price of these commodities is the upward or downward pressure of the price due to the trading demand of the commodity. Thinking this through further, you will see that there are two elements that determine whether your gold, silver, or oil trade will go up or down in a time period. The price will first factor in the value of the dollar as it relates to the fixed value of the commodity. In this example assume that the dollar has fallen in value due to buying and selling in the currency market or foreign exchange market (commonly called **_forex_**) by 1 percent against a basket of foreign currencies. The 1 percent fall in the value of the U.S. dollar will directly affect the price of the commodity. In this example, due to the inverse relationship, the price of gold, silver, and oil _all will go up by exactly 1 percent._

FACT

The value of the U.S. dollar is measured against a basket of foreign currencies. The percentage of each foreign currency in this "basket" is proportionate to the weight of the trading partners of the United States. This value of the U.S. dollar is called the _dollar index_.

The next factor that will go into the price will be the supply/demand functions of the market. If there is a perception of real added demand, the players in the market will bid the price higher. If there is a perception of real lessening of demand, then there will be overall selling in the market and the price of the commodity will fall. This example uses the notion that there are rumblings in the supply chain of oil, causing the perception that the supply of oil will be tight in the near future. Say the bidding demand for oil moves the price up 2 percent. In order to find the new price of a barrel of oil, the market would factor in both price increases—the oil price and the dollar index—and determine a sum increase of 3 percent in the price of oil.

The combination works with lessening demand and a strengthening dollar also, which would cause a percentage move downward in the price of a barrel of oil (this is an example for oil; the same principal holds true for gold and silver.)

A cross in factors can also happen and often does. A cross happens when the value of the U.S. dollar goes in the opposite direction from the demand (second factor). For example, the U.S. dollar may strengthen due to factors in the forex currency market. This would serve as the first leg of the commodity price and would have the effect of lowering its price. When a cross happens, the demand will have an opposite effect on the price of the commodity. In this case the demand would push the price up. If the dollar strengthened by 1 percent, the price of the commodity would fall by 1 percent, and the demand would push the price up by 2 percent. The net effect would be an increase in the price of a barrel of oil (or gold or silver) by a total of 1 percent. Keep this in mind when predicting the price of gold, silver, and oil. The price of each is the inverse to the dollar's value combined with trading demand's contribution.

Seasonal Ups in Commodity Prices

There is an additional factor to the price of commodities that you should be aware of and take into consideration: the effect of the seasons on price movements in commodities. There will be an increase in prices for certain commodities during "peak" seasons; this is in addition to the overall demand for commodities that last for complete investment cycles. The commodities that are most effected by seasonal demand are gasoline, heating oil, grains, and precious metals.

ESSENTIAL

Commodities such as livestock and industrial metals have a demand curve that is flatter than seasonal commodities. This means that their demand is not subject to sharp upturns in price at specific times of the year. Livestock, nickel, and copper definitely have price movements, they just don't have clearly defined seasons.

Gasoline will begin its climb in the spring and peak in the last weeks of summer. It will then trade lower into October and will be at its lowest (baring other factors such as geopolitical events) in late January or early February. Beginning in March, there will be news of upcoming supply concerns and other rumors, all getting the consumer ready for higher prices at the pump in a few months.

Heating oil is the opposite. It will gain in price starting in October and peak in January, then go down in price as the warmer weather of the spring approaches. Adverse weather, cold snaps, and snowstorms in the northeastern United States will cause a stir in the heating oil market and cause the price of this commodity to go up in a hurry.

The prices of grains such as corn, wheat, and soybeans will correlate with the growing season: The supply of these crops is dependent on the growing season. As the volume of the crop is known, the prices will rise or fall inversely to supply.

The price of gold will also coincide with the seasons. Unlike the weather-bound seasons of gasoline, heating oil, and the grains, gold's price will go up in value with the approaching marriage season in India and then continue until the Chinese New Year. More accurately, the price of gold will rise starting in October and gain momentum until it peaks in early April of the next year. The prices that are achieved at the end of the Chinese New Year will be the peak; then it is likely that the price of gold will fall slowly until it reaches a "rest" in the middle of the summer. From there it will ramp up again starting in October and repeat the process.

The price movement of silver will be related to the price of gold. While silver is often called "poor man's gold," on trading days when gold moves up, the price of silver will move up also, and oftentimes by a much higher rate. Silver is volatile and will move two or three times as much as gold will move on the same news and on the same day. This means that if trading news is good for gold and its price moves up 1 percent, there is a good chance that silver will move up two or three times as much, by 2 or 3 percent or more.

This link between gold and silver's prices is also tied to the gift-giving marriage season in India and China. Be warned, however, that if there is very bad economic news and gold prices spike while the dollar falls dramatically, silver's link to gold's price will break: these times often record sharp losses in the silver market. This is due to the fact that silver's price is partially tied to its industry demand. Therefore, if there is very bad news about the economy, the market will assume that there will be little industrial demand.

Up and Down, Good News and Bad

Traders will react to news either by pushing the prices of commodities higher or by "punishing" them and sending prices lower. There are times when economic, geopolitical, or inflation news is good, and this good news causes the prices of commodities to fall. At the opposite end of the spectrum is when bad news is good for the prices of commodities, and therefore good for trading. Knowing the mood of the economic news can guide you as to the direction of whether you should "go long or short" (meaning buy or sell) with your commodities trades.

If you are anticipating bad news, or if bad news is already being reported, then you can read this as a signal to go long (meaning buy and therefore have your trade set up to make money when the price of the commodity goes even higher) the commodities that react well to bad news. At this point keep it simple: Trade only oil, gasoline, or gold. Steer clear of the industrial metals such as nickel and copper. These will take a back seat to the more actively traded "panic" commodities of gold and the fuels.

FACT

You could be tempted to go long silver (meaning you will buy silver), but in difficult times silver will suffer, as traders will shy away from the white metal and put their resources into gold, the yellow metal. The thinking is to buckle up and go along for the ride. If the news is bad, there is a good chance that buys in oil and gold will pay off with profits.

Keep in mind that this is a shorter time-frame perspective. If you are thinking longer term, hold fast and do not be unnerved with the rapid ups and downs in these types of markets. If you are trading on margin, such as with a leveraged ETF, margin account, or futures, make sure you have an extra room for error. You wouldn't want to make a mistake, get caught on the wrong side of the trade, and have your account fall to a value that causes a margin call (a closing of your account by a trading house)! (See "Your Side of the Futures Contract" in Chapter 18 for further information about margin calls.)

On the other hand, when the tone of the news is good, and all are reporting how well the economy is doing, then you can go long copper, the industrial metals, as well as the energies and grains. If the economy were to run perfectly, without excessive liquidity (meaning money supply) and running the risk of excessive inflation, gold would actually not perform as well as the basic commodities. This fact has rung true in the past: In the early 1980s, gold soared to more than $800 per ounce during hard times, and then fell to below $320 per ounce during the good economic times that followed. It can be difficult to predict the price of gold due to its inverse relation to the value of the U.S. dollar. Therefore, if the U.S. economy is doing well, the United States as a nation will attract foreign capital, which will drive the value of the U.S. dollar up and the value of gold down. Keep this in mind, as this is an important lesson to be learned!

Keep Looking for Setups

Looking for setups comes down to cruising the charts, news, and banking websites for signals. It means keeping your mind open for ideas as to what to buy and when. It means having a certain amount of understanding of what it means to trade commodities. This is knowing what commodities are and what they are not. They are part of the earth, they are physical, they are three-dimensional, and they are limited in supply. It is also worth remembering that commodities are not securities like stocks or bonds, which are assets that have their values tied to the cash flows of the companies that issued them.

ESSENTIAL

Looking for setups can lead to a trading lifestyle. It can lead to being so in tune with the economy and the markets that you will become a walking encyclopedia of knowledge regarding central banks, economics, and commodities prices. This knowledge can go from a hobby to a set of skills that will go a long way toward profits.

Once you have a good grasp on the fact that there have been special circumstances used to stimulate the world's economies after the housing and banking crisis of 2008, you will then have a good launching pad in which to begin the accumulation phase of your trading program.

Reading the fundamentals leads to reading the charts, which will lead to getting your money ready to begin buying commodities. If you are trading short term, you will need to work into your day a time to sit down with your computer and look at the charts. It may be a few minutes a day, just before or after work. It may be that you are checking the prices of copper and wheat on the CNBC bottom screen ticker after your mid-day workout at the gym.

If you are a longer-term trader, it may mean cruising the coin shops on days that gold prices take a nosedive. You may get into the habit of "buying on the dips" during these days when coin dealers will be very eager to unload as much gold and silver as possible. You may even notice that the once-coveted yellow metal will somehow seem to be "trash" to people when the NASDAQ or DOW 30 is flying high, while gold still glitters in your eyes!

CHAPTER 7

The Market Speaks—
Can You Listen?

If there is too much information, you may not be able to sort out which information is actually useful and good for you to hear. You can find yourself asking what should you listen to, which information should you trust, where can you find the best sources of trading ideas, and what are the best ways to handle the emotions of trading? You might also wonder how you can trust your judgment and handle your gut instincts. This chapter will help answer these questions.

How Much Information Is Good to Hear?

At this point you could be asking how much information should you be listening to? The best way to answer this question is to remember your trading goals: You are looking for situations in which commodities are priced too high or too low relative to the value of the commodity. This is called **mispricing** and is often caused by emotional events rather than logic. When an investment is mispriced, it offers the trader the best opportunity to get in, to buy, to hold for term (even if that term is a few months or years), and then to sell at a gain on the difference that the investment moved up in price (or down if shorting, that is, selling). That, in a nutshell, is what trading is all about. It sounds simple and it is, really: You wait for the time when the commodity is mispriced due to emotion, get in, and then wait for the other traders of the world to get "over it" so that they will bid until the price of the commodity goes back to fair price.

With this in mind, you will be looking to place a trade in which you can gain upward or downward movement in your favor; that is the only time you will go long, or go short. If the price of the commodity is stagnant, or "stuck in the mud" as they say, by all means, do not get yourself in a situation in which you have bought a load of the ETF or futures and have tied up a lot of capital in the trade. The longer you go holding the product without a rise in price and therefore a gain, the less money you will be making, as that money could have been diverted into a more profitable venture (even if that means paying bills with the money!).

So keep this in mind when you are going over the news and information sources during your trading day. You will buy, hold, and sell. Your only option is either holding longer for more gains or selling in a shorter time frame for a smaller gain.

These concepts are for a trading system that is shorter-term based. The ideas are basic to investing and can be modified for a longer investment time frame if that is what you are building into your system.

Begin each trading day with the idea that you *do not want to spend money on a trade!* Note that this is much different than the "shopping" mentality that most people have when they go into the ETF and futures world.

While commodities offer an excellent investment potential, an ill-placed trade with the wrong price will spell disaster to your trading account. Keep in mind the old trader's adage of "Cash is king," and you will do well. Always think the market through before getting out the calculator to determine how much of this or that ETF or commodity futures you can afford in your account. Cash can become underrated during a heavy market, but in the end, you will always need more cash to buy the next trade. With this in mind, treat your cash as priceless, while you are watching CNBC, reading the brokers' reports, or hitting up the traders' chat rooms. Keeping the perspective that you are "cheap" and not "spendy" will go a long way in helping you interpret the real information in news stories and helping you determine if there is actually a trading opportunity in the making (and not just hype).

ESSENTIAL

Whether you are a short-term trader or are a longer-term investor with an average holding period of an entire investment cycle, the idea is the same: Buy only what has a reasonable expectation of going up in price in the future, period. Don't buy any investment without a clear price path for the future.

Also keep in mind that you should be reading and listening to as many information sources as possible until you build up a base knowledge of the commodities markets. This will give you the best picture as to whether it is going to be a day of trading or a day off. Lastly, news sells, but sometimes there isn't much news, so in order to sell something, the news industry "fudges a bit" and makes a story seem more important than it really is by exaggerating its rightful place in the scheme of things. Be wary of such so-called "news" reports! Always cross-check the idea with your full-service brokers' reports (which for the most part will *not* be biased) and any technical observations relating to the commodity. Remember, *you* decide when to trade with *your* money! Keep the money safe, and only use it on the best trades.

When It's Best to Trade

You should begin each trading day with an overview of what the news is saying with the intent of interpreting how the traders of the world will interpret the same news—remember everyone is looking at the same news and charts. You are looking for emotional plays—the market traders have been either scared or elated by the news and developments in the economy (or geopolitically). You should be looking for the times when the commodity is overbought due to the market traders feeling very good about the future price of the commodity. If this happens, the commodity is most likely due for a pullback and price correction when holders of the older trades sell to lock in their profits, which has the effect of causing the price to fall. The best trade in this type of market is a 2x or 3x "bear" ETF for the aggressive trader and a normal geared 1x "bear" ETF for the more conservative trader.

On the other hand, if traders' (and the public's) reactions have been far too negative to the economic information that is coming from central banks, output numbers, demand numbers, or even a warm winter, then there is a chance that the price of the commodity will have been "oversold." *Oversold* means that there has been a pounding of the commodity in the market leading to a rapid but unfounded price deflation. Keep in mind that these are really the best times to buy into the commodity that is affected. These opportunities come around every month or so, and there is sometimes more and easier money to be made trading during these times of mispricing than there is trying to predict the price movement of the commodity when it is in a normal trading state the rest of the time.

QUESTION

When do you know to sell a winning trade?
Undoubtedly the best way to know when to sell is when things are too good to be true! It is the best time to sell, just as you are convinced that the trade is unstoppable and will never cease to post gains. When you feel this way, by all means sell, take your profits, and run!

With this said, you should go about gathering and valuing your information with different levels of importance. The daily news, CNBC, and what you hear on the train going to work in the morning are good places to start. When commodities make the news or make it to the bus stop, then you know it is a good market to trade in, and one in which to make money. If everyone is talking about how much gas costs, then you better check out the price of oil. Look at what CNBC is saying in its special commodities discussions. Are they "talking it up?" Does it seem that there is a lot of excitement about oil (or corn or other commodity) and how it has risen so fast? Do the commentators ask, "How far will oil go?" If you see these types of words being thrown around, look out! There is a really good chance that oil (or other commodity) has been **overbought** and is ready to come tumbling down after the traders sell off, take their money, and run.

If you see and hear this type of news, why not commit a smaller amount of your capital to a trade that can sit on your books long enough to not cause a problem, but at the same time long enough to be ready when the price of the commodity falls. This is a perfect time for what is called a "set-up" (see Chapter 6) and is actually a trader's dream opportunity. If you are patient, this type of trade can really pay off and add to your overall yearly bottom line. You can make quite a bonus in your portfolio, even if, overall, you are into long commodities with a position in a commodities mutual fund or general commodities ETF. In order to do this you would be tactically short the market only when the opportunity presented itself, meaning you would make small, well-placed trades in a commodity class even in a direction (long or short) that may be opposite your overall thoughts of the entire commodities market.

Trusting Your Judgment

There are two basic forms of information: public access information, such as cable and newspaper reports, and private information, such as the type that is published by your full-service broker or commodities trading advisor. For the most part, public information should be treated as hearsay—*most* of the time it will be correct and presented in a straightforward way. On the other hand, it does lend itself to be interpreted by "experts" who are eager to make a name for themselves, and/or to get their advising services on the map and in the minds of the viewers. With this in mind, you should view public information with a bit of caution. Sometimes the actual data will be turned into information, but with a slant.

There are only three ways that the market experts in the media will spin a story of commodities: buy, sell, or undecided. Once you know that there are only three possible ways that an expert will stand on the price of copper, corn, wheat, gold, silver, or oil, you will be in power! With the knowledge that the advisor quoted in the news has only three choices, you will then be able to sift through the otherwise extra information that will be shared about the commodity.

FACT

Financial analysts use a different skills set with equities than they do with commodities when determining the buy and sell ratings. Investment firms will use a combination of judgment and mathematical formulas to arrive at a "fair price" of a share of stock. The qualitative and quantitative data can solidly predict the future value of a stock.

Remember, you are looking for an emotional reaction to the news. If an expert is talking excitedly about this or that commodity in a manner that seems extra emotional, take notice! The time is right that there is a trade about to come your way. In this sense you will be using the outside public news reports and information sources as a market barometer as to the heating and cooling of that commodity in the traders' minds. It never seems to fail; things that are traded have a tendency to go up and down in price. No matter what "proof" is given for a commodity's price in the market, the commodity will most likely move in the other direction once a resistance point or support level is reached or some other psycho-important price level comes forth. This is separate and aside from the overall gradual price increases in commodities that may naturally come about due to macroeconomic forces such as inflation and a robust worldwide economy. Public news should be accepted simply as a "temperature" and not as the full and only source of information. You should understand that public information and market reports are commonly referred to as **_market chatter_** and are subject to interpretation. So mix these sources with other sources for the best light of trading conditions and when looking for trading scenarios.

Selecting Your Sources for Research Reports

If you have a full-service broker or a futures broker, read your brokers' reports that should be e-mailed to you at the beginning of each day. Or sign up for a demo account at a futures broker in order to have access to their information in the mornings. With most service businesses—and that's what the finance world is, a service _business_—there will be many companies and people who will be vying for your attention and your business. There will be a lot of different places where you can get your information and a lot of people and experts telling you what is a good trade and what is a bad one.

With this in mind, it is best to take your time when looking for a private news source. While the goal of all will be the same, the format, usability, and accuracy among them will be at different levels of professionalism.

Things to look for include early-morning delivery by e-mail, daily reporting, weekly reporting, and a monthly market overview to boot. Most of the larger full-service brokers such as UBS (_www.ubs.com_), Morgan Stanley (_www.morganstanley.com_), Credit Suisse (_www.credit-suisse.com_), and others of this type have a high quality standard for their brokers' reports. Some of these companies even offer two sides of the investing coin on their websites. Your individual account will be shown with research that is geared toward the private client. With the click of a mouse, you can study the research that is written in more depth, research that is written for the institutional investors who use that investment bank.

While the buy, sell, or hold order will be the same in both the private-client research and in the research reports geared toward institutional investors, the depth of the reports will vary. Most private-client research reports will be more instructional in nature. This means the facts will be presented clearly, with a discussion of how each element of the report relates to the final buy or sell recommendation.

So in addition to buy, sell, or hold order, a well-written private-client brokers' report, commonly called a ***research report***, will also contain the reasons why in an easy-to-read fashion. While the whys may be presented in an easy format, the concepts will by no means be at the introductory level. The research will be an intermediate level, which will offer the reader a body of knowledge that can be built upon. Some brokerage houses such as UBS and others take pride in their client services departments, and therefore take great pains to offer more than just advice to their clients. These brokerages think of offering advice with an educational slant. This will be evident in their research reports. When shopping for a source of research, you can go to the brokerage house websites to access and read some of their brokers' reports that have been published on the public access portions of their websites. Of course, this public information serves as a services advertising tool for them, but at the same time will accurately represent what the broker is offering as far as research to its clients.

Using Gut Feelings

Once you accept the fact that you will be trading real money in your account by buying investments that are tied to the prices of commodities, you will need to get to the point where you have a certain sense of security in your gut feelings. After all of the *Wall Street Journal* articles are read, after the last brokerage report is finished, you will need to get to the point where you can decide that it's a good time to trade. Knowing when to trade is never an exact science. It is best looked at as a blending of gut feeling and facts.

You can know the basics of international economics, including capital flows, gross national products, and money supply. This knowledge in itself is very difficult to get a feel for and master. In fact, you may never feel as though you know all there is to know about the fundamentals and all that goes into fundamental analysis. At the same time, you can get into a really good place with your knowledge of technical indicators and your understanding of all of the moving averages, upticks, candlestick charts, and other data that technical analysis can provide.

ESSENTIAL

You can get to the point where you can, with practice, shift on the fly, read the data, build a chart, and interpret your knowledge into a gut feeling. Record your feelings when you see a news story about commodities, and later, compare what you had predicted to the event's actual outcome after it comes about.

The really hard part is putting all of the data, indicators, information, and news together into a gut feeling that says it is a good time to buy. If you are trading copper and copper has just risen from $3.65 per pound to $3.88 per pound, you may think, "Wow, things are good for copper." The next thing in the news may be that China is predicting slower growth in the coming year—not down by much, only 0.3 percent lower than the year before. But the market reacts sharply. This type of news would cause almost every commodity price to fall. The prices of copper would most certainly fall along with oil, aluminum, and steel. In addition to the commodities themselves, the commodity currencies that are traded with China would also move downward. This would include the New Zealand dollar and the Australian dollar.

You then would be faced with the question of whether it is a good time to buy the 2× or 3× copper ETF or the copper futures. You could also consider whether you should buy some of the commodity currency ETF that is invested in the Australian dollar, the FXA (CurrencyShares Australian Dollar Trust).

You may be thinking, "Should I go longer term with my buy in into the overall commodities market, and therefore buy into a general commodities mutual fund?" You will have many choices about what to do with your investable assets.

One of the hardest decisions at this time will be whether to continue to invest in commodities at all. You might consider whether it is time to quit the commodities trading business. The idea may be to get into the hot area of investments, which may be REITs (real estate investment trusts) or technology stocks.

There will be a lot of information telling you where to invest. You will need to check your emotions at the door and proceed as a professional. You will have to use your gut feelings, because after all of the calculations are done, gut feelings are what most professional traders trust the most.

The Emotions of Trading

The emotions of trading with real money have to be tempered. Emotions can ruin an account that is safely tucked away with a cash balance. On the other hand, emotions can ruin an otherwise well-thought-out trade that has temporarily fallen out of favor and is not currently profitable.

Getting to know how you will react to winning and losing in the commodities market takes some training. After experiencing the ups and downs of winning and losing at paper trading in a demo account, you should go slowly into trading with real money.

You can move slowly into getting all of your market and information reading skills into play when you start with a small amount in your trading account. With a small amount of real money, you will still get the experience of the domino effect of a trade. This domino effect is the oftentimes rapid flow of information from reading the news, to studying the brokers' reports, to reading between the lines of the experts on CNBC, and then checking the charts for yourself. Real money (even a small amount) will be your best teacher. You will feel the pressure to buy or sell, and you will feel the emotion that goes with the thought of risk. No one likes to lose, and you may even feel a bit of being burned from trading at other times and in other markets. If you are coming in with a bit of experience, that is good, as you know that money and the idea of making money in the market can lead to strong emotions!

Professional hedge-fund traders use a combination of logic and emotion. These hedge fund accounts use high-powered ultra-fast computers programmed by employees with PhDs in mathematics and statistics to build software. This software is used to back up and quantify the trader's gut feelings before a trade is made.

These emotions are different from the logic of the markets, or better yet, from the logic of a trade mixed with an educated gut feeling of what to do next. Everyone likes to feel as though they are good at making money in the market and good at controlling money electronically. It feels good to enter and exit trades with the profits stacking up. It gives you a feeling of being in control of your financial future. This control cuts both ways, however: Not only are you in control of your buying and selling in the market, you are also in control of keeping your money on the sidelines and in cash if you feel as though something "just isn't right" about the trade. This staying out of a confusing market is actually much harder than you may think. It is easy to trade when there is a clear outcome. It is the gray area of trading that takes the toll emotionally. This is an experience that must be felt with real money in order to be learned fully. Take your time with learning how to deal with the greed/fear emotions of trading. You will fear losing your money while at the same time you may be greedy and think you will win big. This latter emotion spells danger! If you feel this emotional cross, then know that the timing isn't right! You know deep down that the trade isn't good and is risky. In this case a good rule of thumb might be "When in doubt, don't." If this happens to you in an up/down/sideways market, learn to manage the emotions and walk away.

Knowing when to walk away from a trade is key to keeping your earnings! Remember, you are in the business of trading for profit. This means buying and selling at a profit. It also means that once you have the profits in your account, you must work equally as hard to keep them in the account and not give them back by overtrading your account, which more often than not leads to losses.

CHAPTER 8

Profiting on News Developments

When is a good time to buy commodities? The best way to answer this question is to read the news developments of the day and follow the information on news websites and in brokers' reports. In addition to this, you can learn to make observations of inflationary pressure in an economy by searching through the world's central banking websites. The idea is to obtain, analyze, and use information to help you develop an overall commodities trading plan.

Central Banks and Interest Rates

One of the key elements to investing and trading in commodities is knowing and understanding the direction of prices of raw materials. It is safe to say that over long periods of time there will be some aspect of inflation. In today's modern fiat currency world—with **fiat currency** being that the world's money supply is based upon faith and credit—there is a built-in acceptable inflation target of most central banks.

With this in mind, inflation will cause the general prices of commodities to go up over time. This is because there are more dollars and fewer and fewer raw materials to go around, as money is being printed on a constant basis and the world is using up raw materials on a continual basis. The result is more dollars, yen, euros, pounds, francs, kroner, and so on in people's pockets, and fewer and fewer commodities to spend them on; this leads to a natural inflationary spiral. So to put it gently, if the world is in an inflationary spiral, then it is a good time to invest in commodities. One of the best ways to determine if it is a good time to invest and trade raw materials is to look at the websites of the world's central banks.

ESSENTIAL

Searching for information that relates to the growth rates of the largest economies of the world can be difficult. The best way is go to the Bank for International Settlements website. This should be your starting place for data and can be used to lead you to all central bank websites. See *www.bis.org* and *www.bis.org/cbanks.htm*.

Central bank websites are excellent places to monitor the inflation rates of an economic zone. Whether you are looking at the European Central Bank (*www.ecb.int/home/html/index.en.html*), the Federal Reserve (*www.federalreserve.gov*), the Bank of England (*www.bankofengland.co.uk*), or the Reserve Bank of New Zealand (*www.rbnz.govt.nz*), you will notice that the sites will clearly display the inflation rate of the country or area that the central bank services. In addition to this information, many central banks have an inflation target that is built into their mandate. This information will also be clearly marked.

For example, on the Swedish central bank website *www.riksbank.se/en* for December 2011, the inflation target is clearly shown at 2.0 percent while the reported inflation rate for December 2011 is 2.3 percent. While this number is only slightly higher than the target inflation rate, it does show that there is a 15 percent higher inflation rate than the acceptable rate:

$$2.3\% - 2.0\% = 0.3\%$$

$$0.3\% / 2.0\% = 15\% \text{ Over the Target Inflation Rate}$$

Before analyzing this number, switch to another industry-heavy country like China. In the second quarter of 2011, the People's Bank of China (*www.pbc.gov.cn/publish/english/963/index.html*) reported that there was increased chance of inflation, and the Consumer Price Index (CPI) rose 5.4 percent year on year. A ***year-on-year comparison*** (also called a year-over-year comparison) is a comparison between the current month or quarter and the same period from the previous year.

Taking this analysis further, you could then check the inflation rate of a country that has raw materials as one of its main economic components. With this analysis, you could look at three sources: the central banks of Canada, New Zealand, and Australia. A showing of above-average or target inflation in any of these countries would be related to strong economies in their main industries, which in these cases are the export of raw materials.

Buyers of Raw Materials		
Sweden	Heavy Industry Economy	Increased Inflation
Germany	Heavy Industry/High Tech Economy	Increased Inflation
China	Heavy Industry/Light Industry	Increased Inflation
Suppliers of Raw Materials		
Canada	Grains, Gold, Oil	Increased Inflation, Increased Growth
New Zealand	Wool, Grains, Livestock	Increased Inflation, Increased Growth
Australia	Industrial Metals, Gold, Silver	Increased Inflation, Increased Growth

The inflation rates of commodity economies work to be good indicators of inflationary pressure in the raw materials. This is true because Canada, New Zealand, and Australia derive a great deal of their gross domestic product from the mining, growing, and drilling of commodities for export. Second, when there is an increased demand for that country's exports, the demand will have the effect of heating up the economy (and strengthening the currency) of that exporting country.

With this in mind, you should then look for the inflation rate of these three countries. Things to look for are increased inflation beyond the target inflation rate of the country. Other leading indicators are *expected* growth rates of the economy. In this way, the expected growth rate of the economy would be a telltale sign as to what the economy will look like in the next time period (usually one year), and therefore it is called a leading indicator. A **leading indicator** is information and data that indicates the direction the economy will be in the next time period(s).

Looking at the Market for Indicators

When you are performing your analysis, make note of all of your findings. The next step you should look for when performing an analysis of the fundamentals of a country is to look at what the market is saying in general. In a basic sense, the investing media is a **lagging indicator**. In other words, if the information has reached the news in magazines such as *Fortune, Money*, and others, then the trend has pretty much started in that direction, whether it's up or down, and the media is late on the uptake and assimilation of that information: basically, the news has happened already. Some market observers would say this is a bad sign, and that "the time has come and gone to invest in this or that." It would be better to think of it as the slack of the market has been taken up and now the idea of investing in those areas has gained popularity.

In order to understand this logic further it is best to remember that your goal is to capture the gains with your commodities investing: to be in and out of the position as quickly as possible. This idea works if you are strictly trading commodities. That said, it would be better and safer to put your money in any investment just as it started to take off and gain in price (gained popularity!) rather than get into the trade too early and have your investment dollars sit for a long time with flat returns. Keep in mind that the idea presented here is for a "trading account," or a shorter medium-term account. Your plan would be modified if you were thinking of building up your account over time and accumulating commodity assets with a long-term perspective. If you are thinking long term, you would modify the trading tactic to a "position building" tactic, described in the next section.

ALERT

It is best to do some honest questioning about your risk tolerance before you begin to trade and invest in commodities. One of the best ways to tell what risk level you are comfortable with is to look at your trading and investing history. Look at what you have experience with: This best follows your true risk tolerance.

Trade on Momentum

If you are looking to trade commodities in a time period of less than twelve to eighteen months, then the method of "waiting for the news (media) to pick up the story" will work very well for you when making your trades. This, in fact, is a type of **momentum investing**, as you would be getting into a trade as the market was getting hotter, and getting out just as the market cooled off.

The easiest vehicles to use to trade on momentum in the short and ultra-short time periods are oil and gold. These two commodities are the market darlings of the raw materials world. There is something to be said about knowing that you are trading gold when the news station CNBC reports that there was trouble in the European zone, or another major economic issue, as gold can rise dramatically when bad times come.

At the same time, trading oil can be very rewarding when you walk past the corner gas station and notice the price of regular unleaded gasoline creeping from $3.50+ per gallon in the winter to higher and higher prices in the summer. While unsettling to observe, much of the added cost that you and your family will incur with the increased oil prices can be offset by having a long crude oil position. This would be easy to set up. It can be done with the simplest oil ETF. If you set up an oil ETF (or a leveraged 2× or 3× oil ETF), you would profit measurably when the cost of oil went up: step in step with unleaded gasoline consumption. In other words, as you personally use gasoline, you are, in a small way, adding to your oil ETF profits. In this way you could build a hedge against the inflation pressures of your household budget! There will be more information on setting up hedging strategies in the trading section of this book.

Trading with gold and oil can really simplify your investments. Gold is the ultimate safe haven in bad times, and oil is the ultimate industrial commodity because it really gets going in good times.

Building a Portfolio Geared toward the News

You can build a portfolio that is geared toward the news. In this way, you can use the fundamental information that occurs short term to drive your investment decisions for the day. Another phrase for this is ***trading market risk and growth***.

The idea is simple: As the news comes out of Asia and Europe, you would place your trades long or short according to the news of risk or growth. Most market sentiment changes every three days or so, with an overall idea of the direction of the market being positive over time. This means that while it is most likely that the economies of the world will be growing over the months and years, there will be a natural mini-up and down on a week-to-week basis. Again, this is with the thinking that you are interested in doing a more actively managed short-term trading of your account.

As you monitor the growth of the world's economies, as discussed at the beginning of the chapter, this is called your strategy: You will be net long commodities in your portfolio, meaning that the overall dollar position of commodities trades in your portfolio is long, and that you are thinking (in the net amount) that commodities will increase in price. You would then decide the placement of each trade with the market sentiment as it went up and down each three days; this is called your **_tactical alloca-tion_**. This method of actively managing a commodities portfolio can really add to your bottom line over time.

There are tales of gold and silver investors having a strategy of being long in the metals over a period of an economic cycle of five to seven years. With this in mind, they will make trips into their neighborhood coin shop or online precious metals dealers to buy whenever the price of gold and silver dips.

FACT

You don't have to be "loading up" on gold and silver to make this strategy work for you! You can also get into other metals such as platinum and palladium. Although these choices are hard to find from smaller coin dealers, large shops usually have a good supply of these two precious metals. You can add them to your portfolio for diversification purposes.

Since gold and silver have become more and more popular with traders, there is added volatility to the metals. It is common to have gold rise or fall 6–7 percent or more in a one- or two-week period. If you are thinking of building up a physical gold and silver portfolio, then this offers a wonderful opportunity to get into your local coin store to buy a French 20 franc, a British Sovereign, a Canadian Maple Leaf, or other bullion-type gold coins, with the idea being to buy the most amount of gold for the least amount of premium, in smaller, non-numismatic coins.

Just think about it: It is common to have an average 8 percent premium on fractional gold, or gold that is smaller than one ounce. If gold has fallen 8 percent from a week ago, you can now buy the same amount of gold without a premium price that was charged a week ago.

Trading and building up your positions with a tactical viewpoint can get more gold, silver, oil, or other commodities in your hands or in your account at lower prices. Remember the saying, "Gold is gold," and if you liked a quarter-ounce Austrian Philharmonic gold coin at $490 ($1,775 per ounce spot price of gold × .25 per ounce plus a 12.5 percent premium) and a few days later the finance news stations such as CNBC or Bloomberg are reporting that the "economy is strong," "now is the time to buy technology stocks," "unemployment is getting better," and gold falls 8 percent week upon week because traders are rushing into stocks, then the same quarter-ounce Austrian Philharmonic gold coin will now cost you $460 (new spot price of gold $1,633 × .25 per ounce plus a 12.5 percent premium.) The gold coin is still the same gold coin. It will still go into your safe and add to your commodities portfolio.

Trading and Investing with Longer-Term Trends

In addition to the fact that the market sentiment changes every week or so, there is an overall trend that is displayed in the news. This is the greater picture and is usually the trend that lasts over the course of a year or longer. With this in mind, you can think of your trading with the daily and weekly temperature of the market. If this week's market news suggests a cooling off, you might add a bit to your portfolio of raw materials.

When this time comes you might be tempted to back off from commodities altogether, but then the best thing to do would be to switch to your long-term perspective. Your long-term perspective should be built upon the long-term direction of commodities and raw materials in general. This is where the easy part comes in: Commodities are at a point where it is a good thing to buy them. ETFs, mutual funds, gold coins, and silver bars that are bought today will seem cheap in a few years time.

For example, a 1-ounce silver American Eagle, which is 0.999 fine pure silver, sold for $10 in 2004. Now that same silver 1-ounce American Eagle sells for nearly $40 eight years later ($35 per ounce for silver plus the premium). To most people, the thought of 1 ounce of silver selling for $10 when it currently sells for $40 is hard to imagine. The same is true with the ETFs that are built out of commodities index holdings. These have greatly increased in price over the last decade also.

ESSENTIAL

There are factors in the economy today that add to growth in raw materials' prices in the years to come. The long-term trend will be upward for a long time; the only question is, how fast will it accelerate in the future: 5 percent, 10 percent, 20 percent per year? Or more? The time to get into commodities is now!

Looking for long-term news takes a bit of keeping your ears and eyes open. If there is talk of "quantitative easing" or "an accommodative stance" or any other central banking speak of added money supply or lower interest rates, you should make note of it.

Long-Term Investment Plans

As with your short-term buying goals, you also should have a long-term buying idea. Your long-term buying plan may be to increase your overall investment portfolio to double the amount that you are allotting. You may have an objective that you would like to have 15 percent of your stock and bond portfolio in investment-grade 0.999+ gold bars. If these are your overall goals, then keep a notebook or file on your computer of the entire backup of news stories that you see over the months. Refer to these stories and remember what they said that persuaded you that commodities were a good investment when the articles were written.

This is part of your long-term strategy. If you have maintained a notebook of commodities' movement over time in the past, it will further convince you in the future. Think about it: a magazine article stating, "Gold is the place to put your money in 2008 because gold prices will reach $900 soon!" is very convincing when you consider the current price of an ounce of gold. Having this information on hand will go a long way toward persuading you to buy additional amounts of your favorite oil, industrial metal, gold, or gasoline ETF when the prices of these raw materials take a tumble.

A file of past information will go a long way toward keeping you focused on your plan to continue adding to your commodities portfolio and will keep you "buying on the dips" even when the "bad news" for commodities is making people sell.

This week, that week, buying, selling: this is what the professional traders do for a living. If you are thinking of trading a futures account or a leveraged ETF, this is perfect. This trading up and down the price—that is, trading when prices are both rising and falling—creates validity and is what allows for the opportunity to earn money by trading, as the money is made on the upward swing as well as on the down.

On the other hand, if there is a weekly upward and downward movement in the price of a commodity, and you are thinking of your long-term perspective, then this offers a time to build up a position in that raw material.

FACT

Remember, gasoline at the pumps cost about $1 a gallon during the latter 1990s! Since then there has been a huge upward pressure to its price. It is easy to forget what things like oil, beef, bread, and gasoline used to cost. Think of the things in your home: what's commodity-based? Ask yourself, "What did they used to cost?"

Either way, the up and down movement of a commodity price is good: it allows buying opportunities. If you are a long-term investor, keep looking at your database for investments in commodities that have worked out in the past. This upward-pressure environment is the long-term basis of raw materials going up in price. When the ETF or mutual fund you are watching goes down in price due to a "talking down" of the economy, keep the long-term perspective.

Trading with Geopolitical News

There is another situation that can cause a very volatile time in the commodities markets. This comes when there is a political or economic situation that is flaring up somewhere in the world. If the problem is in the oil-producing part of the world, then the price of crude oil, gasoline, and heating oil will go up considerably and quickly. The price for a barrel of oil can rise 5 percent or more in a day and can keep creeping higher and higher until the event comes to a "satisfactory conclusion." Since these international situations can be quite touchy and inflammatory in nature, changes can happen fast, from problem to correction.

It may be a tactical maneuver by a Western military force that resolves the situation quickly. It may be an issue that brews over an entire season concluding during the heaviest travel seasons. For example, it can be a military coup in a country that is an oil exporter, and the civil unrest in that country has halted oil exports. This would drive up world exports building higher and higher until the resolution is met, and then all of a sudden, the price of oil will fall 10–15 percent (or more!) in a matter of a few weeks, often times catching traders off guard. Either way, when this happens (meaning the price of the commodity builds up rapidly and is then set to fall just as rapidly), please, tread lightly! There is money to be made if you are on the right side of the trade. If you are not into the trade and the geopolitical issue has started already, then it may be best to keep out of the market entirely.

For example, if you happen to have a long gold or oil trade on your books, the best thing to do is to keep it without selling right away. Do not fall into the trap of thinking that you should build up your position at this time. There is danger in the market at this time! The big boys will run rampant and drive the market up in a hurry, make their money, and get out just as fast!

These big boys are the traders of the hedge funds and other proprietary firms that use tactics and technology that allow them to be in the trade just long enough to ride the profit wave to the top and then to cash out with a profit just as the situation goes away and the prices collapse.

Bad news is good for people who already hold gold and oil. If you are thinking of getting out of your gold or oil position at a profit during these bad (and high profit!) times, you will need to know when gold or oil is "at the top" and it is time to sell.

The secret to selling during these times is simple: the time to sell is when you have a feeling of "Oh, my! Look how much I've made!" The more excited you are with how much you've "made," then the higher the chance that it will end, the situation will come to a satisfactory close, and the price of the commodity (gold or oil) will fall very quickly. So the answer to "When should I sell?" is best answered by your excitement over your profits. The more you feel you have "hit it big," or "Wow, that's a lot of profit," the more you need to hurry and close out the trade and take your profits.

ALERT

Hedge funds are highly leveraged pools of assets. Most hedge funds are unregulated by government agencies; this means that hedge-fund managers have a broad range of tactics they can use to amplify the returns of hedge funds. Hedge funds generally involve a leverage ratio of 4:1 or higher plus the leverage that futures can offer. This leads to big pressure on the prices of commodities.

Remember: most financial advisors quote 10 percent per year as an acceptable gain on a stock investment and 6–7 percent gain per year on a well-balanced investment. If you are nearing this rate and only a few days or a week have gone by, then you have made a year's returns in less than a week! Take it and run! Do not wait for more. Profit is profit and sometimes you get lucky: You are in the right trade at the right time. Keep in mind, the more thrilling the profit, the closer it is to going the other way and entering into a zero-gain situation. Keep an excitement meter in your head: You're thrilled? Then *that* is the time to sell!

CHAPTER 9

Active Commodities Trading

This chapter will tell you what goes on in the typical trading day. If you are a long-term trader, you need to know what to expect as you go about building your positions over the months. You will also need to know how to keep your assets in your account and not get into the habit of buying and re-selling too often. If you are a short-term trader, you need to know some risk-management techniques that professional traders use.

A Typical Trading Day

Trading is like a sport. It takes training and skill to sit at the computer and hunt out opportunities in the market that allow you to make money buying and selling commodities. There are many ways to trade, including the fast-acting and highly leveraged commodities futures markets, the 2× and 3× leveraged commodities ETFs, commodity currency ETFs, and commodity currencies in the forex market. In addition to the faster electronic trading is the slower-paced trading of physical metals by timing the market and making the trip to your neighborhood coin dealers.

No matter what type of trading you are doing, you will basically fall into two categories: the first is the more paced, easygoing style of those who are building up their positions slowly. These traders are those who would like to have a huge pile of gold or silver coins, a great number of commodity ETFs in their IRAs, or even buckets of copper pennies in their basements at the end of five, seven, or ten years.

These are the long-term traders, and if you are among this type, you will not be too concerned with the hour-by-hour trading ranges of copper, wheat, or corn. You would be interested in the estimated price of cocoa in the next six months, as this would indicate to you whether it is a good time to load up on this commodity now, or whether you should shift your focus to another commodity such as an industrial metal like nickel or copper.

You may also decide that industrial metals are not the place to be in the medium term. This would come from an idea that the economies of industrialized nations of the world are slowing or are currently in a recession, and therefore the demand for the "building metals" would be slowed for some time.

FACT

Knowing what to invest in for the long term can be easy to determine. In order to get the best long-term picture of what will perform best, remember that gold performs well in good times and bad, grains and livestock are neutral, and the industrial metals do best in good times.

So what is a typical trading day for those who are building up a position for the long haul? The answer is that the days are more or less blended into research days and weeks, as the time to actually act on the economic information comes more slowly, with employment numbers, central bank meetings, and inflation figures coming out staggered every few weeks.

With this in mind, you may be able to monitor your whole commodities portfolio and look for buying signals in a calm, relaxed manner that would include scanning through a paper version of the *Wall Street Journal* as you wait in line for your favorite coffee drink at the local café, or taking a relaxing break and casually "checking in" with the economy as reported by CNBC.

Some of the best ways to accumulate assets like commodities that are geared to be under inflationary pressure is to buy and walk away. This is one of the key factors in building up a long-term position in the commodities. Rest assured, they will go up in price. Your best bet is to buy what you can afford, and then keep it out of your mind for several months.

Living the Long-Term Trading Life

If you trade long term, then think long term. This is how you will surely pull ahead. Don't get into the habit of checking the balance of your online brokerage account every night when you get home from work. If you buy what you can afford, or even just a bit under what you can afford, you will not be put in a position in which you will have to hurry up and resell the item (gold or silver) or mutual fund, commodities ETF, bag of pennies, etc., in the near future.

The idea is that you are able to afford to let the capital that is tied up in the investment "sit and rot" while you go about your life, golfing, dining out, shopping, sailing, fishing, poetry writing, dating . . . whatever!

With this method of investing you are set to go out and buy your gold-filled watches, your 90 percent silver quarters, your $50 per month into the DWS Enhanced Commodity Strategy C (SKCRX) mutual fund, or a series of small "timed" purchases of Oppenheimer Gold & Special Minerals (OPGSX) mutual fund. You will be able to buy into the market at your leisure. The key is your intent: You have intent to accumulate. If you are buying less than you can afford, you will not be tempted to sell off at the first sign of oil, corn, or copper weakness. By the same token, if you have just purchased less than you wanted to or could afford, you will have some money left on the table to add more to your positions.

ESSENTIAL

If you trade long term, it doesn't matter that the ETF, mutual fund, or silver prices have gone up 3 percent, 5 percent, or 7 percent. If you are in for the long haul, you may not even notice the rise in price. The idea is to tuck the investment away for at least six months (better yet, twelve months) before looking at its new value.

Keeping track of the market is not the same thing as keeping your hands on your goodies, though. Some people have discovered that electronic accounts that allow them to log in each day and check each day's cumulative value have lead to "overtrading." Frequent peeking at your account can be a downfall—but there's something about the digital format of the Internet and money that charms people, perhaps the desire to "move money around at the click of a mouse."

How to Prevent Overtrading

This "overtrading" is precisely why the private money managers and wealth advisors do not allow their high-net-worth clients to trade online. It is true, the bigger your account in dollar terms, the more you will get guidance from your financial advisor. If you just bought 100 shares of Power Shares Commodity Index ETF (DBC), your advisor would go to lengths to talk you out of reselling it too soon. In fact, he would argue strongly against your overtrading, as it looks bad for advisors (in the financial advisory business this is called the "churn and burn"). There is no such advisory oversight, or discouragement, when using discount brokers such as E*TRADE or Scottrade. These online brokerage accounts are 100 percent self-directed and therefore 100 percent self-destructive!

Keep a Paper Trading Log

One of the secrets to keeping your commodities treasure in the treasure chest and not allowing yourself to constantly run the risk of clicking the button to sell it at a moment's notice is to keep a paper trading log. In today's world of online banking and trading, a paper trading log is a quaint idea. Small hard-bound, three-ring binders hold loose-leaf homemade or preprinted trading diaries in which to record the date, number of shares, and symbols to track over time.

Additional information can also be recorded. Keeping track of big news stories that went along with that day's trade as well as the level of the indexes such as the Dow 30, NASDAQ, and some of the European indexes—such as the CAC 40 (France), DAX (Germany), FTSE 100 Index (London Stock Exchange)—can be added next to the trade information.

Refer to this paper journal when you are thinking of your commodities treasure (paper ETFs, mutual funds, stock; exchange traded notes, or physical gold, silver, and copper.) The act of referring to the book allows your mind time to absorb the skills needed to slowly accumulate the metals, oils, grains, and livestock assets. If you are a long-term investor, you will find this process quite helpful in keeping *your* assets your assets and not your *sold assets.*

ALERT

If you are keeping a paper journal to track your trading, don't pass up the opportunity to record as much information as possible. In addition to dates, number of shares, and symbols, write down any pertinent information related to the trade. One good example is to record the weather conditions in the northeastern United States when you are trading heating-oil futures or energy ETFs.

With long-term investing in commodities, time in the saddle is the key. The longer you hold on to the item, the more it is worth. Your best bet is to buy and hold for a long, long time. If you feel the need to fiddle with your account, refer to your trading journal. Write some notes; plan your next buy in. But never, never sell too soon!

The Short-Term Trading Day

On the other hand, if you are the type of trader who would like to be short term in your time frame, then you will have a much different type of trading day. Your days will be spent in the electronic arena, either day trading commodities futures contracts, leveraged commodities ETFs in your online brokerage account, or spot trading of oil, gold, or silver in a forex trading account.

Either way you look at it, if you are trading short term in minutes, hours, or days, then you must rely on the most up-to-date news. This news will be the source of your short-term fundamental analysis. At the same time, you must read your broker's reports every morning when they are e-mailed to you. Next, you also will need to keep up the same amount of long-term fundamental analyses that you would if you had a long-term perspective.

The facts are, if you are trading in the short term, you run the risk of losing sight of the long-term direction of commodities in general. You may be looking at the charts and technical indicators with such close intensity that the 50-day/200-day moving average becomes a 10-day/20-day moving average with a time frame of 30 seconds or less!

FACT

When performing technical analysis, make sure you are using different time-frame charts with the same time-frame indicators. Matching indicators will show the right information for your trading horizon. For example, you wouldn't want to look at a weekly chart of one-hour increments with five-minute indicators!

If you are short term, keep in mind that you are really long term also. You trading day will then be spent with the overall assurance that there is light at the end of the tunnel during hectic trading days, and the light at the end of the tunnel is the steady creeping up of prices of commodities.

So the question is, what is a typical trading day like? Rest assured, it is not time spent in a hot house trading pit like is shown in the movies. If you really want to know what it "looks like" to be a professional trader, then keep your eyes open for guest speakers on CNBC. CNBC oftentimes carries special reports from the "trading desks" of some of the major players such as Royal Bank of Scotland (RBS Marketplace at *www.rbsm.com*) and Wells Fargo (*www.wellsfargo.com*).

Next time you see these views of a large trading room, notice how quiet and controlled the environment is; it is not loud, crazy, or haphazard in any way. These offices are dealing with large sums of money, and they buy and sell huge amounts of investments each day. Since they are in the business of making profits, the traders will enter and exit out of trades with an accuracy and a precision that is uncanny in nature. Sure, the money is not "theirs" and therefore they can have a calm, cool, and collected posture about them. However, for the most part, traders will be paid extra for the profits they make, and they will be let go if their losses are too great. Too much risk, too much loss, out they go. The trading world and investment banking world is small, people know one another, and for the most part, reputations are at stake as much as the amount of money that is on the line.

These observations can be beneficial to you as you begin your short-term trading endeavors. Keep in mind that you are the boss when it comes to your trading. You can run it like a business, and therefore think of it as a business that has the purpose of earning a profit. If you keep in mind that you are trading real money and that you are doing it for financial gain, you will naturally slow down your decision making to the point that each trade is weighed.

You will be spending your days reading the early-morning edition of the *Wall Street Journal* over coffee. You can switch to the before-market reporting on CNBC while you are getting the kids off to school. After warming up to the markets and getting your bearings, you might read a daily report on corn futures, for example, that your broker has e-mailed to you.

Reviewing all of the news that happened the night before, you switch on your computer and log in to your trading platform. Quick checks of the long-, medium-, and short-term charts get you to the point where you will know if it will be a good day to trade and make money in the market.

Using Basic Risk Management Techniques

Once you have decided that it is a good day to trade, you will then go about building and tearing down positions with a turnaround time of minutes, hours, or days. You will be looking for setups that will allow you to earn a small percentage rapidly and to build up the profits of the account over time.

If you decide to trade short term, knowing how to use some risk management techniques will go a long way toward keeping your trading in a profit zone. One of the basics of risk management is the process of building the position in smaller segments over equal sets of time.

The best way to do this is to build up your position into a commodity by buying three equal-dollar-sized bites. If you are trading leveraged ETFs, then the best way to do this is to divide your trading account in thirds. Next, divide one of the thirds into another set of thirds. These amounts will be the money that you will use to buy into the leveraged ETF.

The number-one reason that traders get into trouble is that they commit too much capital into one trade and do so at one price. In other words, if you have set aside $2,500 that is separate from your main long-term portfolio of stocks and bonds, you run a much riskier game if you bet $2,000 or more with one purchase.

This is because what usually happens is that once you commit the funds to a purchase, there always seems to be a reversal in price, and your newly acquired ETF (or futures) will go down in price (or up if you shorted with a bear ETF.) It never seems to fail that no matter how well you have plotted and planned and placed the trade at the perfect point, there will soon be a point in the market where you wish you hadn't bought so much, or wish you hadn't even bought the ETF, stock, or future at all!

Try to match the time of the one-third purchases with the planned length of the trade. If you are planning on a 5 percent rise in price over a week, then time your one-third purchases every other day. This time frame would act as an effective price-smoothing technique.

It seems to be the law of the land that the price will rapidly move in the other direction once you buy. To counteract this seeming law of nature, you should always under-commit your capital so that you still have an adequate supply of cash on hand. This cash on the side of the table is often called "dry powder" by professional money managers and is used as a reserve cash stash to buy more when the opportunities present themselves.

A good trader can't always predict the direction of the market. You most likely will be the same. You will use all of the fundamental and technical indicators to time the best entry point to buy into the commodity you are trading. Once you have bought it, you own it and at that price. If you have spent all of your money on that one trade and it happens that the price of the commodity moves against you, then your back will be against a wall, and the only way out will be to sell at a loss, or to hold and wait for a price reversal. Either way you will have no real proactive way to have a bit of insurance against the inevitable up and down of an active market.

If you follow the one-third of the one-third plan, you will have plenty of cash on reserve to make another buy in the commodity at the new price level. In this way you will be spreading the buy in points across time, and therefore buying in with a dollar cost-averaging effect. This dollar cost-averaging effect is called **_pyramiding_** and can be done in sets of three or five buy-ins depending on the length of time you plan on holding the position.

If you are thinking a day or less, then three entry points with no more than one-third of your overall trading account will go a long way in keeping your position in the green, meaning the position will be able to be closed out in the future at a profit. Change the number of entry points to five entry points (one a day) for five days for a position that is built up over a week. If there is a fast-moving market, you might also consider dismantling your profitable position in three or five equal trades, each as they move into a profit position. You could casually point and click your way to profits at the different prices.

More Ways to Manage Risk

The net effect of the equal buys and then equal sells is one of a smoothing of the profits against the jagged ups and downs of commodity prices in the market. This profit smoothing will make for slower, steadier gains, with less chance for losing trades. The one-third of one-third pyramiding is an excellent way to incorporate some risk management into your trading. It is a proven technique that is used by professional traders; it is easy to learn and easy to build into your trading system.

Diversification

There is a second method of risk management that is based on the theory of diversification. One of the best methods to keep yourself out of trouble when you are trading is to spread your money around and if possible, counter at each position with an equal but opposite reacting position. This is the idea of hedging your bets, or better said as "Don't put all of your eggs in one basket."

This is a very basic idea of diversification within an asset class. In other words, once you have your main portfolio set aside with mainstream stocks, bonds, CDs, and cash, and you have determined what percentage of your overall portfolio will be used for trading, you would then diversify within this trading account.

Using the previously mentioned one-third of one-third method, you would carry the idea further by using two-thirds of your entire account for trading and one-third that would always remain in cash. In this way you begin the diversification strategy as the U.S. dollar will be rising and falling more or less inversely to the motion of the price of commodities in general.

FACT

The risk management department of professional trading houses has the task of giving individual traders the signal when they have built up too much leverage or are under too much risk in their positions. These risk managers will constantly monitor the trading desk to help keep the traders out of trading trouble.

The idea is that one-third of your trading account will be firmly entrenched in movement which is opposite to the general movement of a long position in all commodities. This is true because commodities prices are based upon supply and demand, as well as the fact that a falling value of the U.S. dollar will also add to the strengthening in the value of the entire commodity index.

Dividing Into Thirds

You should think of ways to hedge your trading account and not put all of your trading eggs in one basket. Just as a three-legged stool will not rock (as opposed to a four-legged stool), a trading account that is built into three elements will be very effective in adding stability to the value of that account. The best way to do this is to divide the account into thirds. One third will be in U.S. dollars. The second third should be in a traded, but less so, nonleveraged commodities index ETF. The key to this is that you will be gaining long-only exposure to the entire commodities market in a way that is cost effective and slow to react to the market. Since you are looking for stability and a sort of anchor in the trading account (but without the low yield of cash), you will still have exposure to the overall commodities market. At the same time, the final third of your account will be tactically deployed in both long and short positions, as is done by buying 2× and 3× bull ETFs when the market is set to move up, and then switching to 2× and 3× bear ETFs when the commodities market is set to move down.

The net effect of the one-third of one-third concept with a third of the trading account put into cash, a third into long-only index ETFs, and the last third into bull and bear leveraged ETFs (in three separate buy-ins) leads to a very solid, secure trading account that offers enough latitude to make money in up and down markets, but at the same time is not unnecessarily too risky. The upside of this trading account arrangement is slower, steadier gains. Risk management does not have to be made of complex mathematics and computing. It does mean watching your buy-in amounts and building your account so that it is equally balanced as to offer overall stability.

CHAPTER 10

Risk and Commodities Trading

You're thinking that trading in commodities might be for you, but what about the risks? The first thing you should know about any investment is what are the risk issues. The second thing you should consider is how to go about reducing these risks to an acceptable level. Sometimes it means switching to trading a safer investment vehicle rather than one that is higher risk. Other methods include having a long-term approach and a long-term investment time horizon.

The Elements of Commodities Risk

What are the risks to commodities investing? There are many, but with proper risk management technique, much of your risk can be minimized. Putting it simply, there are three types of risk, and they overlap one another.

1. **Liquidity.** The risk that your investment will be tied up for a longer time period than was anticipated; also that it will be difficult to convert your investment back into money at the same or higher price than it was purchased at.
2. **Volatility.** The risk that the price of the investment will go excessively up and down over the time of the investment.
3. **Timing.** The risk that is related to the difficulty in determining the proper entry price point of an investment and the proper exit point.

The basic idea of the risks of commodities is the fact that it is very hard to determine the right price at which to buy the gold, silver, oil, or corn and still be able to sell at a later date for a profit, or in the worst case, at least to break even and get out with no loss. With this in mind, remember the base idea: You are to buy low and sell high. While this may be a simplistic point of view, this is actually the opposite of what most people do with their investments. While the quest for capital gains is what drives most people's search for the right trade and the right investment at the right time, it is actually very difficult to "break free" from a return that is above the basic risk-free rate and earn an above-average return on your investments. This means that while it is occasionally possible to earn 5 percent, 7 percent, 9 percent, or even higher, being able to do this consistently takes practice and patience.

With traditional investments such as stocks (equities) and bonds, there is a natural up and down to the market. This is due to the fact that investor attitude can change from day to day, week to week, season to season. It can be a fact that if you are investing in the overall equity market (represented by the S&P 500), you have a really good chance to be investing in a time when the market will be flat over an investing cycle of seven to ten years.

FACT

This means that if you invested $1,000 in an S&P index fund as an initial deposit, you would have made nearly 0 percent returns for the entire ten- to twelve-year period. If, on the other hand, you were to buy into the market at the highs of the time period, you would have actually lost money, because the average price of the index fund's shares would have gone down over time. This is also the case with most other investments; hence, you have the built-in risk of investing in general.

The other risks come up when the investment that was bought at a high price must be held on to for a long time before selling: This occurs when the investment was bought at a higher price and then a lower price sets into the market, which would cause a loss if the investment were sold at the lower price. This is timing risk.

The third risk can come when the volatility of the commodities market whipsaws your trading efforts. When oil is up and down $5, $7, or $10 within a few days, it can be very difficult to decide at what price to do your buying and selling. If you are in a trading day that shifts up or down according to news events, then watch out! Your well-thought-out trades can lead to very poor trading ideas in a few hours or days, and thus to heavy losses.

Determining Your Risk Tolerance

After considering the basis of the risks involved with commodities trading, you need to consider your individual risk tolerance. If you have a high risk tolerance, this means you will be able to accept a chance that your investment may lose money when sold, or that you would be able to sit with a trade or investment that is "underwater" (losing) for as long as it takes for the trade to turn around and return to a profit.

If you have low risk tolerance, then you are the type who would be concerned with reconverting your commodity investment back into money at all times, with zero loss and preferably with a profit.

That is pretty much it; with commodity investing the risks are simple. In fact they are much easier to manage and plan for than the risks involved with equities.

ESSENTIAL

To put it simply, risk all comes down to timing. You must ask the question: How long are you willing to tie up money in your commodities investment? First determine your timing tolerance. Then look at your commodities investing products and endeavors to match that timing tolerance.

If you are thinking you need your money to be into a trade and out of a trade within a week, then you will need an investment that can get you in to for a profit and get back your cash that fast, like an ETF or 2× or 3× leveraged ETF, as these are cheap and easy to trade with an online discount broker. If, on the other hand, you are looking to build a longer-term portfolio of a few years or even an entire investment period of five to seven years, then you have higher chances of success and therefore can take a greater risk. Time would be on your side. If this were the case, you could consider a long-term buying program of ETFs, stocks of commodity companies, gold miner mutual funds, etc.

Time works to your advantage with commodities, because the world is in a period when things are starting to heat up again in terms of commodities consumption. After a strong setback from the housing and then banking crisis of 2008–09, the world's building, manufacturing, and spending in general slowed down considerably. This leaves the door open to those who are willing to get into the commodities market after a setback and just at the beginning of another time of acceleration in prices.

In addition to the fact that the world's economies have seen setbacks in recent years (and are ready to pull strongly forward), there is the point of the added money supply in the pockets of consumers and companies that will go toward bidding up the prices of those commodities. It will be as if there is a double whammy on the prices of material goods and commodities in particular. The world's largest economy, the United States, had set forth two quantitative easing sessions (QE1 and QE2) as a result of the banking and housing crisis, and followed it in September 2011 with Operation Twist (which some called QE2½), which greatly added to the amount of U.S. dollars in circulation; there is talk from the Fed that there will not be a reversal of this QE until late 2013–2014. In fact there is often the mention of a "continued accommodative stance" by the chairman of the Federal Reserve, which causes the market to wonder the length of time that the Fed will take before once again "tightening" the money supply. Other nations have followed suit: Great Britain has gone to the full QE3, and due to the Euro Zone's Greek crisis, the European Central Bank could ease as well.

Monetary Easing, Inflation, and Risk

Monetary easings are slow to take effect. Once they are in full swing, they are very slow to curtail the effects of inflation they have been known to cause. The best thing to do to profit from them is to have a long and sustained buying program that includes acquiring commodities and commodities-based assets.

The effect of natural inflation built into the system; the "bottom," if you will, of an economic cycle (due to the fallout from the banking and housing crisis); and the added liquidity and money supply might very well lead to a situation of high prices for investment-grade raw materials. If you have a long-term approach, the investment risk of commodities will be minimized due to the "creeping up in price" effect of the grains, the metals, and the energies.

FACT

Keep it simple: If you have a long-term time horizon, then buy a commodity index mutual fund or ETF, visit your local coin shop, and sort your pennies. If your time horizon is short term of a few days or weeks, then trade the 2x or 3x leveraged ETFs or get into futures trading.

Keep this in mind when acquiring gold, silver, commodities mutual funds, and commodities ETFs. These are long-term "buy and hold" investments, while futures and leveraged commodity ETFs are short-term, trading investments.

So the question of risks associated with commodities investing can be minimized by the following ideas: The first is that the natural inflation effect that is built into the world's economic systems will act as to cushion the ups and downs of raw materials' prices. Unlike equities or stocks, there are no balance sheets to copper, cocoa, corn, nickel, gold, or oil. These raw materials *can't go bankrupt*! These items are simply mined and used up. While there might be times when the use of natural resources is slower than normal, the fact remains that there are limited amounts of these materials and unlimited amounts of money that can be printed and put into circulation.

With this being said, it is natural that there is a bit of inflation, even in normal economic times. With the current economic situation of quantitative easing, which is actually a method of putting additional money into the system, and the bottom of an economic cycle, the argument can be made for the possibility of added inflation in the future economic cycle. If the argument is accepted, and you believe that there is a chance of more than the usual price pressure on goods and services in the future, then you would conclude that for your portfolio, commodities investing is a good place to consider.

This inflation pressure can add up to be quite a bit in the coming years; add to it the growth that comes after pent-up demand and this leads to higher prices in commodities. These facts can lead to pressures that alone can absorb the risks that are often associated with commodities investing. In fact, most of the risk that is commonly associated with this investment class is actually the same risk that is associated with futures trading. Since futures trading is a form of highly leveraged, fast-moving trading that can involve margin calls and therefore the added risk of wiping out the equity of a trader's account, most risks of commodities can be removed by buying and selling more traditional investment vehicles.

Managing Volatility Risk

It can be quite easy to withstand the normal market ups and downs of a broad-based commodity index ETF or a mixed asset commodity mutual fund. Even if you only wanted to invest in a certain type of commodity such as industrial metals, energies, or grains, you can find an ETF that will fit you. You can then buy it and hold it without the use of leverage or margin in your brokerage account. This means you can own the commodities cheaply and be taxed efficiently (because you would minimize your taxes with a buy and hold strategy) and your investment portfolio would not be too greatly disrupted by a 10 percent or even 20 percent reduction in the price of raw materials in the ETF or mutual fund. If this happened, you would just wait until the price rebounded before selling.

ALERT

Remember, a loss in a trading account is not really a loss until it is *realized*. This means the loss is a loss of actual money only when the asset is sold at the lower price. If the price of the asset moves up and down over the weeks, this is *unrealized and not yet an actual loss*!

The net effect of the inflationary pressure of the future and the bottom of the economic cycle of the present can offer quite an incentive to add to your commodities holdings in your investment portfolio. In fact, it can be said that if you steer clear of higher risk trading of futures and leveraged ETF trading on an hourly and daily basis, and you instead buy a more traditional type of investment vehicle, you could reduce the risk of commodities investing considerably.

In addition, you could further reduce your risk by buying the target investment in small amounts over the long term. The added volatility of the commodities market can lead to very good buy points for those that have a bit of money set aside. You could have a goal to put 10 percent, 15 percent, or greater into gold and silver coins (or oil ETFs or a commodities index mutual fund), then you would find ample opportunity to "buy on the dips." You could always keep just enough of your last buy in reserve for the next buy. Then you will always have money to log into your online brokerage account and buy a few shares of an ETF or go to your neighborhood coin dealer to pick up some silver. In this way, you can "load up" in commodities in a hurry. You would be surprised how fast a concentrated effort to accumulate silver coins (or a mutual fund) will add up to a large quantity of the commodity. If you are going for the physical metal, copper, gold, or silver, you will see the metal pile up fast! In fact there is kind of a magic to this type of accumulation: There always will be money to buy more if you have a goal to buy more. Over time this can add up a very large position in the commodity vehicle of your choice!

Leverage and Margin Risk

There are other factors that can add to the risk of a commodities portfolio. One of the highest levels of risk with commodities comes when you trade with leverage. **Leverage** means that you are basically using a charge card to borrow money to invest with.

How it works is this: you place a certain amount of collateral in a brokerage account. The laws and regulations of the time will determine the amount of leverage you can use to borrow against your equity in the account to result in a larger purchasing power in the account.

The leverage, or borrowing, ratio is lower for equities investment (such as stock and ETFs) and higher for futures investments. The rule of thumb for stock and ETF investments is a 1.5× allowable margin. This means that if you have $1,000 worth of energy ETFs in your brokerage account, you will be able to borrow an additional $500 against the $1,000 to equal $1,500 worth of buying power. This is what is meant by a 1.5:1 margin limit.

On the other hand, if you are trading commodities futures with an online trading account, you will be allowed to have a 10:1 to 20:1 margin limit. This means that in order to buy $1,000 worth of futures contracts you need to have $100 in your margin account for a 10:1 ratio and $50 in your margin account if you are trading with a 20:1 margin.

While the leverage amount in the equities account is only 1.5:1, you can afford the chance to buy more commodities stock or ETFs by a means similar to that of a credit card. Just like buying on a credit card, you buy commodities stock or ETFs and pay a monthly interest on the borrowed amount, at a rate that usually is cheaper than an actual credit card, and 6–8 percent higher than the prime rate.

With the added margin and buying power comes the chance to leverage the amount of your return on investment. For example, say you put $1,000 in a margin account and you buy $10,000 worth of corn futures. If the price of corn goes up 2.5 percent, your $10,000 account will be worth $10,250, or a $250 gain. This $250 gain was made on only a $1,000 cash investment: this means an actual return on investment of 25 percent!

FACT

While stock margin accounts are 1.5:1, and futures margin accounts can go as high as 20:1, forex accounts, or currency accounts, can go as high as a 50:1 margin. Keep this in mind when you consider trading indirectly in commodities by buying and selling commodities currencies discussed in later chapters of this book.

Leveraged trading may seem to be quite the money maker, and if you learn to trade the futures market, it can be a very good return on your investments. On the other hand, if the corn futures in our example went down 2.5 percent, your loss would be 25 percent and your $1,000 cash margin account would be now worth only $750.

Since the margin sword cuts both ways, it should be only used with experience, and only when you are most assured of the direction of the commodities you are investing in.

At the same time, leveraged ETFs that are set up to be 2× or 3× bull and bear funds can offer even greater amounts of leverage in a very concentrated amount of purchasing power. While normal margin on equities and ETFs is 1.5:1, these leveraged bull and bear ETFs offer 2:1 and 3:1 margin ratios in both directions. This means if you bought one of these funds in the "bear" direction, you would make 2× or 3× the amount of the "short" return. Funds that are in the "bear" direction are set up to make a profit when the commodity falls in price. They act like a "short" position but are simpler to buy than a true short in a brokerage account, as you do not need any special type of brokerage account to trade them.

These can be especially profitable during times when there has been an ultrashort-term run up in the price of the core tradable commodities, such as gold, oil, silver, and copper. If you are thinking of trading with the bull and bear 2× and 3× ETFs, it would be best to stick with these core commodities: They seem to bear the brunt of the ups and downs when the market is hyped up and trading rapidly. Make no mistake: there is real money to be made in these leveraged ETFs. In fact, these have become the market darlings of independent individual traders of today.

Dollar Cost Averaging to Reduce Risk

Dollar cost averaging is one of the best ways to limit your risk in commodities. To use a slower, sustained, more casual approach afforded by dollar cost averaging means you will be thinking of the long term—of long-term ways to increase the amount of these investments. You will also be more resilient to downturns in the market and will be less willing to sell off your investments when the season is off or when the prices are slightly lower.

The key to dollar cost averaging is to establish a goal of setting aside a certain amount per period to buy into your preferred investment. The secret is to put away the same amount each time, regardless of the current price at the time.

This way, if you were to put $100 into a commodities mutual fund, you would be buying $100 worth each month; sometimes the price of shares in the mutual fund would be lower and sometimes the price of shares in the mutual fund will be higher.

ESSENTIAL

The best way to think of dollar cost averaging is to think of your over-all commodities investment as a commodities accumulation over time. With this thought, you naturally will be slower on the uptake with your buying into the commodities equities, mutual funds, ETFs, and physical metals. A relaxed stance is best when getting into a commodities investment program.

If the price of shares in the fund is lower, you would be buying more shares for your same $100 as the price of each share would be less money. If a share was originally $25 per share and you invested $100, you would get four shares that month. If the next month the price of commodities fell, and therefore the price of the shares of the fund fell to $20, you would then get five shares for the same $100 investment. On the other hand, if the shares in the fund were more expensive (due to higher commodity prices), you would be buying fewer shares for the same $100.

This is the essence of dollar cost averaging; buy more shares when they cost less, and buy fewer shares when they cost more. When you do this over a long time period, the effect is a lessening of risk due to the fact that the price paid for the asset will be averaged over time, which has the effect of smoothing out the highs and lows of investing. In this way, the risks of commodity investing can be minimized: The timing of your investment and the volatility will be reduced by dollar cost averaging.

This method works best with mutual funds but can be modified to use for ETFs and gold and silver bullion and coins. If you are thinking of dollar costing with these, then think ETFs that are priced less so there is the effect of buying more shares, and buy smaller 2½- and 5-gram gold bars and small 1-ounce silver coins.

CHAPTER 11

Crude Oil Trading

This chapter will introduce you to the basics of crude oil trading. This includes learning how to include crude oil and its derivatives such as gasoline and heating oil futures and having the patience to get to the point that you can read the market. Once you have this skill, you can reap a healthy profit. Of course there are easier methods to gain profits with oil commodities, such as when you learn how to trade the leveraged bull and bear 2x and 3x ETFs.

The Elements of Oil's Price

Crude oil can be one of the heaviest hitters in your commodities portfolio. Crude is traded all over the world, but the main exchanges are in New York and London. The volume of oil trading and the daily dollar amount that is traded is larger than any other traded commodity. One of the reasons for this is that oil fuels the engines of the world's economies. Shipping, transportation by airplane, and driving by autos are fueled by oil. Additionally, oil is used in the manufacture of plastics and other goods.

The basic elements that make up crude oil's price are supply estimates, demand estimates, and the U.S. dollar index. All three tug and pull at the price of oil. When there is excess supply, the price of oil will drop; when there is excess demand, the price will rise. The third factor in the price of oil is the value of the U.S. dollar. The value of the U.S. dollar is measured by the U.S. dollar index. When the value of the U.S. dollar goes up or down against the value of other currencies, the price of a barrel of oil will move in the opposite direction. The price of oil has an inverse relationship with the value of the dollar. This is true because the value of a barrel of oil will remain constant as the value of the dollar moves up and down.

FACT

Many traders follow the supply and demand numbers for crude oil. This information is then used to estimate the best prices at which to buy and sell crude oil futures contracts as well as crude oil–based ETFs. The most reliable source for this data is the U.S. Energy Information Administration (*www.eia.gov*).

Investing in Oil

The price of crude oil is watched closely by the investing community. Since oil is a key ingredient to the workings of the world, it makes sense to have a percentage of your commodity holdings invested in oil.

If you are investing in a broad-based commodities mutual fund, then most likely the fund will have a high percentage invested in crude oil and gasoline futures. Make sure that the fund is invested in crude oil–related company stock. This would include companies such as BP and ExxonMobile, as well as some of the lesser known companies such as Anadarko Petroleum Company and Hess Corporation.

You might also consider a mutual fund that has exposure to the oil services companies. These companies are the builders of oil pipelines, oil rigs, and hubs. Many times stock analysis will heavily recommend companies in this service industry as an accent to a portfolio of pure oil stocks. This is true because these companies are directly related to getting future oil out of the ground; it is believed that this industry would be very profitable during times of high oil prices.

Trading Oil ETFs and Leveraged Oil ETFs

You can also get into ETF and futures trading if you want to build a position in crude oil. Of the two, buying and selling oil-based ETFs is the easiest and the simplest. If you are building a commodities position in your investment portfolio and you are doing so by including different layers of assets, then you should make sure that a larger percentage of those commodities assets are oil-based.

You may choose to have the core of your commodities portfolio be a broad-based commodities ETF or mutual fund. You could then amp up the returns of this core portfolio by going long and buying bull oil ETFs. You may even have a core portfolio of ETFs that you are slowly adding to over time, but you are "trading" the leveraged bull and bear oil and gasoline ETFs. These leveraged ETFs are perfect for daily trading. They offer 2× and 3× leverage as compared to the regular ETFs. This means that if you buy a bull 3× crude oil ETF, you will make three times the upward percentage of crude oil's price. In other words, if crude oil is really on the move, and goes up 2 percent in one day, then your 3× bull ETF will move up three times as much, or 6 percent, and a 6 percent gain in an ETF is a healthy profit, to be sure. Another thing to consider is that these gains will come from oil and not from trading some newbie or high-flying stock that may be "here today and gone tomorrow." Oil is a key component to the world's economies; in fact, some say oil is more precious than gold. With this in mind, it can be said that if you are trading oil, you will be in business for many years to come, and profits will await you!

ESSENTIAL

It is a good idea to divide your investment portfolio into three sections. The first would be your core portfolio of stocks and bonds. The second would be your core commodity mutual funds. The third would be your trading portfolio: this would be your leveraged commodity ETFs.

In addition to the leveraged 2x and 3x bull ETFs are the leveraged bear ETFs. These "bear" investment products are structured internally to short the oil market. In other words, they have a reverse structure that allows them (and you) to make money when the price of the commodity is going down. The bear oil ETFs will short the market exactly as if you were shorting the market in a futures account.

Both types of ETFs in the leveraged and nonleveraged forms are tied to the value of the NYMEX traded crude oil futures. While it can be difficult to manage a futures account, with their high levels of margin and daily settlement, much of the same effect can be made by trading these ETFs. Leveraged and unleveraged bull and bear ETFs are very simple to use once you learn how.

Practice Bull/Bear Leveraged Oil ETFs

The best thing to do well before committing any capital to a leveraged ETF is to do some practice trading, more commonly known as "paper trading." Paper trading in a demo or practice account would allow you to get the nuance as to the directions that ETFs go to during a busy trading day. You may be eager to put your money on the table, but trading should not be looked at as entertainment. It would be better to look at trading as though it were a sport. When you look at trading as a sport, you would train for an event, which includes some stretching exercises (think warming up.)

Think about your trading as the extreme sport of rock climbing and you will have a good analogy as to how to get up to speed for the event of trading. You will also need a good idea of what types of equipment it will take to climb, especially safety equipment.

Taking the analogy further, you would not only need to have the strength to climb (the available cash to make the trade) but you also would have to exercise in order to have full range of motion of your legs and arms so that you could reach high and low and feel for all of the nooks on which to get a hold and pull yourself up.

In addition to this, you would need to know the strategy of how to make a hard climb easier by taking the right path up the side of the cliff, and you would have to know how to handle the ropes and such that would prevent you from coming down when you didn't want to, or worse, having your climb end in disaster!

ALERT

When there is real money on the line and there is the chance of winning big, get into it and play with all of your heart! You will find that you feel the same when you win money in the market as when you are playing a sport, or worse, as you feel when winning at a casino!

Think of your strength as your money; your flexibility as your wits in knowing how to build long and short positions, allowing you to make money in up and down markets; the strategy of making a hard climb easier by knowing to not trade when there are no trading opportunities or there are too many issues in the market (leading to no clear direction of a trade); and knowing how to use safety equipment. These considerations would be the same as your knowing how to use your trading leverage effectively and also how to use risk management techniques such as hedging.

The best way to learn to get a feel for how these 2x and 3x ETFs move in a fast market is to get some experience trading them without running the risk of losing real money. Some say you will not learn as much doing it this way because there is no actual chance of financial pain and therefore your risk taking and risk aversion will not be based upon fact, as demo accounts are funded with play money.

Real Pain and Joy from Practice Trading

The facts are that the pain of loss in a demo practice account is real because it makes you realize that you don't know what you are doing when you make a mistake. Rest assured, you will feel very bad when a practice trade is made carelessly and it comes down around you in a quick minute. Even though the money in the practice account is not real, it can be very intimidating to lose money in a trade that you made on your own. This is actually the best way to learn. Make trades and win big. Then take your good feeling of winning into the commodities market and place another trade that loses. It is a key requirement to know what it feels like to lose after a feeling of winning.

Cavalier attitudes and hubris are two of the biggest reasons that people fail in the market in the long term. This is normal! It is almost a requirement and a rite of passage for traders in the market to make gains until they are so confident that they begin to lose. Everyone goes through it. Once you feel the pain and embarrassment of loss, you will learn to take your trading seriously enough to not take unnecessary risks. These are the laws of trading, and it is best to learn the lessons with play money in a demo practice account. In a practice account, the emotions of the ups and downs of trading will be real to you, while the financial loss will not be real. In the end, the lessons of trading will be learned in a most cost-effective way.

Practice with Bull and Bear ETFs

You should take time to learn how these leveraged ETFs move in all kinds of markets. You should learn how these oil futures based ETFs react when the news of the world is making people nervous and the price of oil jumps. You should also learn how these ETFs react when the world's news is making the oil traders sleepy and the oil price stalls, or even falls by a few percentage points.

ESSENTIAL

The bull ETFs and the bear ETFs are quite popular with professional traders. Across all classes of investing, these funds offer the most bang for the buck and with the most control. It is no wonder why these ETFs account for much of the trading volume in the stock markets.

It is good to get a full range of experience trading both 2x and the 3x oil ETFs. In addition to the normal direction bull ETF, you may want to try your hand at shorting the market and begin an experiment of trading the bear ETFs.

While it is easy to conceptualize how these funds move up when the market moves up, it takes a bit of practice to estimate when they will move up and by how much. Shorting the market can be one of the most unusual things: News media such as CNBC will have reports on falling prices, and you will see the ticker of the commodity moving deeper and deeper into the red. At the same time, you will see your profits growing and growing! It is even stranger when you are seeing the multiples that the leveraged oil ETFs will provide. Take some time learning how this relationship works before you commit any real money by using a demo or practice account.

Most brokers offer access to a free demo account in order for their customers to try out investment ideas. If your broker doesn't offer one, there are several providers on the Internet. A Google search for "demo stock trading" or "virtual stock trading" will lead to results that will link to offerings.

Oil Information Websites and Investment Banks

Keeping an eye on oil supply and oil demand will go a long way toward keeping you going in the right direction as far as placing your crude oil trades. Whether you are trading futures, oil-company stocks or ETFs, you should be reading sources of information that allow you to get a bird's eye view into the world of oil and oil production.

Sometimes it takes a deep review of leading industry websites such as the *Oil & Gas Journal* (*www.ogj.com/index.html*) or reviewing websites that are geared more to the investor such as Hart Energy Publishing's *Oil and Gas Investor* (*www.oilandgasinvestor.com*). These sites offer a lot of hard-to-find information all in one site. Additionally, they include links to other advertisers' sites that can then lead to even more information.

Many of these separate advertisers are offering structured private-placement investments, or even shares in oil companies that have yet to produce a single barrel of oil. While this may seem like a long shot to some investors, others may see the value of getting in on the ground floor of a proven well that is just about to pump; that is, of course, if the geological surveys are good, and so on. Some of the ads are for smaller investment banks that specialize in studying and valuing oil and gas concerns; these banks will be happy to discuss with you the deals they are currently offering. Shares are usually an offering of equity for a larger buy-in of $25,000 or more. Also, some of these smaller outfits are only building one or two oil wells, and with the value of oil being near $80 and above, and the well scheduled to be a shallow well that yields 40–50 barrels per day, the total equity side of the deal may be valued only in the $10 million to $20 million dollar range. Compare this with BP's total equity valued at approximately $138.4 billion (at this writing), and you get a better perspective of the relatively small potential of one of these small firms!

ALERT

Learning about your chosen commodity will help you know when is a good time to buy and sell, and at what price. Keep going over brokers' reports and industry websites to keep your knowledge fresh. Things change quickly in the commodities world; learn to keep up with the most current information.

A good dig deep into the Internet with key word searches such as "oil and gas investment banks" will yield good sources of information for you as an oil and gas investor. For example, Simmons & Company International (*www.simmonsco-intl.com*) is an investment bank that specializes in the oil and gas industry. Going to these sites is like looking at the flip side of the investment coin. The first type of investment banking site is the type that has offerings for their clients. If you want to invest with a small investment bank that has a deal—called an offering—for you to invest in, then you would contact that bank. You could then buy the shares of the offering through your full-service broker such as Merrill Lynch, Morgan Stanley, or possibly a full-range online broker such as Interactive Brokers (*www .interactivebrokers.com*), which is an online trading platform and brokerage that offers worldwide access. Interactive Brokers is often used by smaller hedge-fund managers themselves, as IB offers access to several markets, including futures, stocks, mutual funds, forex, etc., as well as access to many exchanges worldwide. Think of using a broker such as this if you are getting into trading and like the flexibility and offerings of full-service brokers, but prefer to do more on your own.

The Anatomy of an "Oil Deal"

So one side of these types of investments is when the investment bank makes an offering to the public, or to a client who meets certain financial criteria in the investment banking business; this is called the "sell side" of the business.

Before this can happen though, deals are sought out and the investment bank seeks to assist the oil-well owner in her need for raising cash to build the well and to get that well's oil to the market, thereby making the investment pay off; this is called the "capital raise," or simply the "raise."

Most well owners will have an option to the land and will need to buy the parcel first. Second, they will need the cash to get up and running and into production. This money may be needed in stages, such as three payouts (or more) as opposed to a full lump-sum payout. If the investment bank works with the well owner, the bank may arrange different financing options, such as a combination of equity, debt, and options, all done in an effort to get enough money to the well operator to get her equipment in the ground, built, and to secure purchase orders from buyers. This part of the deal making is called the "buy side."

Most of the investment banks discussed in this section are smaller, boutique banks. Many also offer wealth management services; if you are interested in developing a relationship with one of these investment banks, ask your financial advisor for a recommendation. While all such banks will be licensed, not all boutique investment banks are equal in quality.

During this process, the investment bank will be looking for investors such as you. After a consultation with a selling investment bank, your lawyer, or your full-service financial advisor, you may decide upon investing with the first, second, or third stage of financing, and is divided according to the ongoing development of the project. In other words, the project may start with a need for geological surveys and such, which would be the first stage of financing. As the project progressed to actual production there would be a need for additional injections of capital, each at a predetermined stage of the project's development and capital needs. You may be advised to buy a mixture of mezzanine debt that pays a high rate of interest (short-term startup debt to be repaid after a capital raise) and equity (ownership and a claim to the profits) as well as an option or warrant on the production of the well. Both options and warrants allow you to share more of the profitability of the well after certain minimum barrel production levels are met. Your buy-in of the offering can get quite complex, and rightly so: You are dealing with custom-made financial products with extreme flexibility for both parties' needs.

There may be different deals in the works at the same time for the investment banks. Your financial advisor may recommend staging your investment, spreading your investment moneys across many different well locations, and also diversification across different physical locations of the well projects. Further diversification can be achieved by selecting different investment banks that are offering the deals; especially so if the deals are set up as venture capital. This venture capital, or VC, usually comes with the venture capital company inserting its own management team into position on the ground offering hands on guidance on location (as opposed to managing remotely from an office far away!) to help manage and run the day-to-day finance and operations of the new business you just invested in. If this is the case, divide your money between several VC managers and invest in different wells that are managed by different VC management teams. This will bring an added level of diversification to an otherwise concentrated position in gas and oil investments.

CHAPTER 12

Gold and Silver

This chapter will introduce you to two of the classic forms of commodities: gold and silver. Gold and silver are in a special class of commodities due to the fact that they have historically been used as money. After reading this chapter you will have a better idea of the role of gold and silver in the world of commodities trading and commodities investing. You will also be introduced to the basics of precious metals buying and selling.

Gold and Silver Are Money

The precious metals of gold and silver have been used as money for centuries. If you go into some of the higher-end coin dealers located in the world's major cities, you may still be able to buy a Lydia, which is what some consider the first coinage. These odd-shaped bars of a gold/silver alloy are marked with the king of the time's sign: a roaring lion.

Even today, the leading rulers and governments hoard gold and issue gold and silver coins with their symbols on them. The United States has the American Gold Eagle and American Silver Eagle bullion coins, marked with the national motto. Great Britain is still minting the Sovereign Gold coin, with the bust of Queen Elizabeth on its face and the symbolic St. George slaying the dragon on the reverse. Other countries have produced or are still producing their versions of gold and silver coins, including Canada, Australia, China, and Austria.

If you look to the past, gold was the base measure of money. Things were simple then: There was a certain amount of gold and silver in the treasuries of home countries' vaults. This gold and silver was minted into coins of a certain weight and purity called *fineness*. These coins were then used throughout the land to buy goods and pay for services.

Sometimes the lower-priced services were also paid for with copper or iron coins. This money served as the backbone of the payment system. Bread, livestock, or a hearty drink at the local pub were paid for with coppers, or some version of today's penny. Some of these coppers were actually quite large, as they represented a buying power that was much more than today's pennies. Nonetheless, the common man and woman made most purchases with these smaller-value coins.

FACT

When Michelangelo painted the Sistine Chapel between 1508 and 1512, he was paid in the gold coin of the day. According to banking records, he was paid a total of 3,000 gold ducats over a ten-year period. With a ducat being 0.1106 ounces of gold weight, at today's gold value, this amounts to approximately $115,000 per year!

On the other hand, large purchases, such as horses, land, or building supplies, and other capital goods cost quite a bit more than could be paid for with the pennies. These good were often paid for with the larger valued coins, which were made of gold and silver.

Back then, the value of gold and silver didn't change much over time. Because this was true, there was usually a fixed amount of silver coins per one gold coin. In other words, if you had a house built and it cost you 100 gold coins to build it, you could pay with a combination of gold and silver. The number of silver coins would be fixed to the number of gold coins. Historically, this amount was 20:1, or twenty silver coins to one gold coin of the same weight.

More important expenses or investments had to be paid for with gold coin, and only gold coin. This was especially true when tribute was to be paid to a leader, such as a duke, barron, or monarch, because these leaders were continually building armies and fortifying alliances with other leaders. Since gold was the best and most accepted form of payment, these leaders were continually striving to build gold reserves.

Gold as a Method of National Payment

Later on, in the late nineteenth century and into the mid to last quarter of the twentieth century, gold was still being used by the developed nations as a payment system. The presidents and prime ministers of these countries were often concerned about building gold reserves in the name of their home country. In this case, gold was again used to pay debts between countries at the national level. It was also used to back up the value of the other form of money: paper currency.

Paper currency came about for merchants who were traveling and needed money that was easy to transport. Gold or silver was to be deposited in a vault at a private bank. Notes would then be drawn against the deposits. The system began to work very well once many merchants were on board, leaving a great number of notes in existence, and therefore gaining widespread acceptance by all members of a town or country. This method was started in the Italian Renaissance and quickly spread to other developed trade centers such as Flanders and Bruges, in the modern Netherlands and Belgium.

As the city-states developed into full countries, national notes replaced the private bankers' notes as a medium of exchange. The paper money was still backed by the gold and silver that was in treasury vaults of the kings and queens of the countries. At this time, some countries adopted a central bank method of dealing with the gold and silver deposits and the issuing of the notes against them. Some say the world's first central bank was the Bank of England, born of a charter by the king to issue notes and pay interest against bonds that were sold in an effort to pay for the then cash-strapped British Empire.

During times of extreme stress, such as during a war, the only thing that can be used to pay for goods is gold and silver. This was evident during World War II when both the Axis and the Allies nations where using gold to pay for their war supplies. Huge amounts of gold flooded into the United States and Switzerland at this time and, for the most part have stayed there to this day.

ESSENTIAL

Before 1965, dimes, quarters, and half-dollars were made of 90 percent silver. Ninety percent silver U.S. coins can still be bought today at coin shops and are priced by the face value. In other words, ten dimes will be worth the same as four quarters and two half-dollars: they all add up to $1 face value of silver, or 0.723 ounces.

There was even a time that it was declared against the law for people in the United States to own gold. Gold coin was to be given up, and in exchange, replaced with the equivalent amount of paper money. New storehouses for this domestic gold hoard were built at Fort Knox, while the gold reserves of the Allies nations were to be held at the deep-down subterranean vaults of the Federal Reserve Bank of New York.

After a time of great stress and economic battle over the fate of U.S. gold holdings, the U.S. dollar was no longer directly convertible into gold by foreign trading partners. The "gold window" was closed in 1971 by President Richard Nixon, meaning gold and the dollar were no longer directly linked in value. Since then the value of gold was as gold itself and was allowed to rise or fall in value according to the market.

Who Buys Gold and Silver Now?

You may ask, Who buys gold and silver now? The answer is simple: the same people who bought it years ago. Most people who are buying gold and silver these days are all thinking alike: that gold and silver will rise in value as the price and purchasing power of the U.S. dollar, the euro, and the British pound go down.

The future of these three currencies holds the future of the prices of gold and silver. If more money is to be printed through quantitative easing at the central bank level in the United States and Great Britain, as there has been already, and you add an influx of the European Bloc currency, the euro, the net effect is a kind of seesaw on the price of gold and silver. Add to this any geopolitical unrest and zoom! The price of gold and silver is set to rise quite high.

The key elements are twofold. First, gold and silver are priced in these three currencies (the U.S. dollar, the British pound, and the euro). Therefore, no matter what country you are in, and no matter what currency they use there, when you go to buy an ounce of gold or silver, the price will be quoted in dollars, euros, and pounds. Thus you would have to convert your home country's money into one of these three currencies, and then use this money to buy the gold or silver.

If you were buying a gold coin in Canada, Dubai, or New Zealand, you would go to the gold dealer in your area. He would have gold prices quoted in the three currencies, along with the conversion rates of your home country in those three currencies. There may be a slight difference between the conversion rates of New Zealand dollars to U.S. dollars and New Zealand dollars to euros (as dictated by the forex, or foreign exchange market.) No matter, you would choose most the cost-effective conversion. There would be no need to actually convert New Zealand dollars to U.S. dollars and then take the paper U.S. dollars to the gold dealer for cash; rather, the process would be done automatically and in one exchange of New Zealand dollars to gold.

This is the process that goes on over the entire world when gold and silver are bought and sold. If there is a quote of a commodity in dollars, euros, or pounds, and these currencies fall in value due to inflation (caused by overprinting of money, a heated economy, or ultra-low interest rates), then the value of the commodity will rise in price at least in proportion to the inflation.

QUESTION

Is gold considered money?
Some people say no, gold is not money, because gold can't be used to buy goods and pay for services. On the other hand, why is gold being stored up in the treasury vaults of the world's largest countries? Why is it that the United States holds gold on its balance sheet, right along with euros and Japanese yen? What do you think?

To put it mildly, there is only so much of a commodity to go around. There is only so much gold in the world. The supply of gold is so limited, it is said that 95 percent of the gold that has ever mined since mining began (3,000 to 4,000-plus years ago) is still in existence and in the hands and vaults of investors, central banks, and jewelry wearers. This is significant, as it shows the limited supply of some commodities to the extreme.

Valuing Gold and Silver in Today's World

Since gold will continue to be of limited supply, and the amount of money (especially dollars, euros, and pounds) in circulation has risen and is expected to rise, then it is safe to assume that the price of this limited supply of gold will go up. It is a simple matter of more money chasing a limited amount of gold (and silver). It is true that there is additional gold and silver mined each year, but in a bull market for these metals, the demand will exceed the limited supply of mined metal, creating upward pressure in its price. Additionally, as the price of gold increases, mines will be more profitable, and more effort will go into the business of mining for gold. At the same time, if there was a future situation in which the money supply were to go down—say, with central banking action, a raising of interest rates, or falling worldwide economic activity—then there would be a case for falling commodities' prices.

If interest rates of the U.S. dollar were to climb substantially, investors would clamor to buy U.S.-denominated long-term debt such as T-Notes (Treasury notes) and T-Bills (Treasury bills). The switch would be on, as traders would see the beneficial tradeoff of gold and commodities to the high interest of paper investments such as the long-term debt. This is what happened during the 1980s when there was widespread inflation in the United States. The price of gold rose to very high levels and then fell as the interest rates were hiked.

The central bank manages things a bit differently these days and there is new management from time to time. This, along with the special circumstance of the banking crisis and housing crisis, should result in an interesting outcome.

FACT

If it is gold you trade, you are in one of the most exclusive "clubs": This group includes some of the heaviest hitters of the investing world as well as some of the biggest central banks of the world, including the IMF, or International Monetary Fund. You will be in good company for years to come!

Your best bet is to continue to trade and invest in such commodities as gold and silver. At the same time, take heed of the past and learn the lessons of the present. This means keep reading the websites of the central banks for information and become a "walking encyclopedia" on the commodity of your choice. If you were to pick only two or three things to trade or invest in your commodities portfolio, then gold should be on that list for sure.

Silver's Returns Can Accent Gold's Returns

If you invest in gold, then you should consider that many people add 20–30 percent of their gold holdings to be made up of silver. A large percentage of the value of silver is based in its industrial demand, including its use in electronics, photographic supplies, and jewelry. Since this is the case, silver prices will react very positively when gold rises in value, as silver too is a precious metal. On the other hand, when there is very bad geopolitical or economic news and the world's economies are believed to be slowing down, then gold prices will rise but silver prices will fall.

This decoupling of price is getting more and more apparent as the economy reacts to both good and bad news coming out of the last recession. With this in mind, add to your gold holdings with a "timed" approach. This means buy on the dips, and hold the silver as a "return enhancer" to your precious metals portfolio.

ALERT

Many times gold will go up 1 or 2 percent while silver skyrockets up 3 percent, 4 percent, or higher that same day. The futures market for silver is small and reacts sharply to news and trading pressure, both up and down. Keep this in mind if you are buying silver in the electronic spot market, physical market, or futures market.

The price of silver is still related to the price of gold, much like it was many years ago. While the price of an ounce of silver used to be at a ratio of 20:1, meaning twenty ounces of silver to one ounce of gold, the ratio changes as much as the ratio of dollars to gold does.

The price of gold to silver has changed to the point where it is accepted by traders to be at a ratio of 50:1. This means that when the price of an ounce of silver is $35, the price of an ounce of gold will be 50 times higher, at $1,750. This is the benchmark ratio. Knowing this will help you time your buys of gold and silver. Websites such as Kitco (*www.kitco.com*) will list the gold/silver ratio. Get into the habit of checking this frequently.

If Kitco is reporting a gold/silver ratio of 50:1, gold and silver are said to be neutral. If the price of silver rises at a higher rate than the price of gold rises, then the ratio will fall. A ratio of 40:1 or less is a strong buy signal for the price of gold to rise. This means that if silver was $35 an ounce and the gold/silver ratio was 40:1, then gold would be priced at $1,400. In this case, since in the modern age of gold and silver ETFs and easily accessible electronic spot trading, the gold/silver ratio should be 50:1, traders all over the world will be predicting either a fall in the price of silver to $28 an ounce ($28 × 50 = $1,400) or a rise in the price of gold to the new level of $1,750. At this point you will have to decide whether you are a bull or a bear for gold! If you are checking the gold/silver price ratio then you would also be checking other sources of information to develop a really clear idea of where gold or silver prices will go to next.

Ways to Buy the Metals

Once you decide that you are a bull for gold and silver, you next need to decide how you would like to invest in them. There are several ways, but these methods of investing and trading can be divided into two basic methods: electronic trading or physical trading.

Electronic Trading

The electronic method includes futures trading and ETF trading. Futures trading is especially difficult and is covered briefly in this book. You will most likely find trading commodity futures to be a daunting task. In fact, when most people think about commodities, they think of the high-risk, high-stakes game of futures and options on futures trading.

Most likely you are a more traditional investor. If so, or if you would like to gain exposure to the commodities market, and gold and silver in particular but on a more conservative, easier-to-handle method, then precious metals can be bought and sold in a way that suits your style. These methods include buying ETFs. The gold ETF known as SPDR Gold Shares, or its NYSE symbol *GLD* (*www.spdrgoldshares.com*), is one of the best known and most widely traded. Shares of GLD represent 1/10 of an ounce of gold. The prices of GLD move up and down in step with the fluctuating spot prices of gold.

ESSENTIAL

Since GLD shares are fully registered securities, they are able to be held in any normal brokerage account. Just like a share of Microsoft (NYSE: MSFT), GLD shares can be traded and held in all manner of brokerage accounts including IRAs, Roth IRAs, SEP accounts, and 401(k) accounts.

Additional methods include trading of gold and silver in the spot market. This is most easily done with a forex trading account that allows metals trading. If you live in the United States, the forex dealer will *not* allow leverage in this type of trading; rather, the buy will be at a 1:1 ratio, without the heavy leverage of your normal forex trading. The benefit of this type of trading is that you can buy gold and silver with currencies other than the U.S. dollar. You may, for example, buy your gold or silver with British pounds, with euros, or with more exotic currencies such as the Singapore dollar. This may benefit you if you are building a currency play into your overall investment portfolio.

Physical Trading

Some say the most active method is to go out and buy actual precious metals. This may take some getting used to—getting in the car and driving to the local metal or coin dealer and paying for old silver dollars, gold bullion bars, or vintage foreign gold coins. Most of this buying will be done with cash, and then of course you must deal with the issue of where to store the coins and bars once you have them. Buying silver will also keep it interesting as you can collect different types of "art bars," or bars that were made years ago as advertising or handouts from different companies, including local banks. There is collecting of varieties of gold coins too, as there are many different types, from many different companies.

Lastly, you can search through old shops and antique shops looking for gold and silver jewelry that can be bought at prices that are cheaper than the melt value of the gold or silver objects' content. (See Chapters 15 and 16 for more information about physical investing in gold and silver.)

Any way you look at it, gold and silver can be added to your portfolio with ease. Keep this in mind when thinking of building up a position in these two precious metals. Also keep in mind the ratio of gold to silver and the fact that gold has been and is used as a resource for central banks. Think of this as proof that you have a wonderful investing opportunity with gold and silver.

CHAPTER 13

The Industrial Metals

While gold and silver are considered to be precious metals, steel, aluminum, nickel, and copper hold their value because they are used in the manufacture of durable goods. For this reason steel, aluminum, nickel, and copper are called the industrial metals. If you are considering gaining exposure to the commodities market, you should certainly add a portion of the industrial metals to your commodities portfolio. This chapter will give the ins and outs of these metals and how best to make money trading them.

The World's Building Supplies

The ***industrial metals***—which include steel, aluminum, copper, and nickel—are the most important components for building in the industrial world and in the industrial world's economic machine. These metals are more important than gold and silver as far as adding to the economic well-being of the world's economies that are dependent on manufacturing. China, Japan, Germany, France, Belgium, and the United States (among others) are drawing a great deal of their economic might from the fact that manufacturing is a component of their economies. In addition to the end users of the world's building supplies, you also have the countries in which these metals are mined. These countries benefit from price increases in the industrial metals because foreign capital will come into the country to pay for the metals that are shipped out to the end users.

For the most part, steel is the most heavily traded and used industrial metal. It is used in the manufacture and building of most everything that is durable, including ships, buildings, autos, and appliances. The trading and use of steel is followed by aluminum and then copper. Aluminum is used in the manufacture of lighter-weight components of cars, airplanes, and small electronic equipment such as iPads and laptop computers. Copper, on the other hand, is an excellent conductor of electricity and therefore is used in modern electric motors of electric cars, as well as in appliances, home and office wiring, and plumbing.

FACT

While steel is the most widely used metal in the world, it can be expensive to trade electronically. This is because there is only one steel futures contract available to trade in the United States. This steel futures contract is listed on the CME Group marketplace in Chicago; it is not an E-mini contract but a full-size contract only, which means that it has a high cost due to its large size (as opposed to an E-mini contract which is for the smaller trader.)

If getting in on the commodities boom means adding the industrial metals to your portfolio, then it is best to get a broad knowledge of the industries and metals that you will be investing in.

Steel

China is the world's heaviest producer of steel, followed by its neighbor Japan. Because of China's ever-growing economy coupled with its first-rate status as a steel producer, there is a flow of iron ore into China from countries such as Australia that extract it from the ground. The raw iron ore is shipped into China from exporting countries; it is then turned into steel and steel products. This finished steel is then shipped out as the country turns from importer of iron ore to exporter of steel. This steel is shipped throughout the world and sold as an inexpensive alternative to the more expressive steel that is made domestically in the United States, Luxembourg, Germany, and other places.

In the past it was considered a bit unpatriotic for a manufacturing company to buy inexpensive "cheap" steel from Asian manufacturers. The import of this steel has been beneficial, however, as it led to improved steel manufacturing methods in countries like the United States, resulting in smaller, cleaner, and more efficient steel plants in these nations. This has by no means meant the return of all of the steel-mill jobs in the U.S. Midwest, but it has meant better-run companies and better technologies used in the manufacture of steel products.

Aluminum

After steel, aluminum is the second most used metal in the world. Unlike steel, which is made of iron and carbon, aluminum is itself an element. Extruded aluminum and cast aluminum products are used as the lightweight elements of the bodies and motors of cars, airplanes, and rail cars. In addition to the skeletons, body panels, and power plants, aluminum is also used in the fasteners and foil manufacturing industry. This means aluminum is used in nails, screws, and the rivets that hold the body panels to the frames of these cars and aircraft. Aluminum is also used in the auto, shipping, and aviation industries, and in packaging.

If the idea of investing in aluminum is in your sights, there are a few information-rich websites you can go to in order to learn as much as you can about this important metal before you begin investing. One of the best websites to look for information is the International Aluminum Institute (*www.world-aluminium.org*), which offers all of the latest aluminum mining, aluminum inventory statistics, and alumina productions numbers by quarter. The institute's website also gives what it calls a technology roadmap with all of the latest production processes, etc. This is an excellent source to use to learn all about aluminum, how items are processed, as well as what estimated demand for the future will look like. Lastly, there is a link to its members, which represent 80 percent of the world's aluminum production. Located at *www.world-aluminium.org/About+IAI/Members,* this part of the site is an excellent place to begin looking for companies that work in aluminum. This information is important if you are searching for a company to invest in if you want to gain exposure to the aluminum market but don't want to play the futures market.

ESSENTIAL

Gaining exposure to the industrial metals market by investing in the companies that mine and produce these metals can sometimes be the best way to get commodities in an otherwise conservative investment portfolio, as they are less risky than a futures market or even industrial metals ETFs.

Other sources of information about aluminum include The Aluminum Association's website, (*www.aluminum.org*). This site is much more interactive, with several sections of news for the different manufacturing areas including recycling. It also features a bookstore and a Q&A section.

Nickel

Nickel is another of the industrial metals that can be traded. One of the main uses for nickel is in the making of stainless steel. Most of the nickel that is used in the steel mills throughout the world is mined in Australia and Russia. While nickel is an industrial metal, its price is not as easy to predict as the prices of steel and aluminum. Perhaps this is because nickel is an additive to the stainless-steel making process, and therefore not as a major player in the commodities world as are steel and aluminum. On the other hand, if you were to think about a well-diversified commodities portfolio, then a percentage of this investment would include nickel. This is why the larger, better known commodities indexes include nickel in their composition. Trading nickel can be difficult, as the only futures nickel contract that is available is traded on the London Metals Exchange or the LME. Due to the trading regulations of the LME, there are very few futures dealers that offer U.S. investors access to trade on the LME. An alternative to direct nickel futures investing would be to invest in the Australian dollar. This would work as the value of the Australian dollar would climb as the price of its exports (including nickel) would rise in value on the open market. More of investing in commodities currencies is discussed in a later chapter.

Copper

Copper is one of the basic materials that go into construction and building worldwide. Almost half of the copper produced goes into the building and construction industry. This is one of the reasons why the price of copper is so closely related to the health of the economy. In other words, if the world is experiencing a building boom, then there will be a rise in the price of copper. If there is economic news that the world's larger economies will be experiencing a period of increased growth, then traders who specialize in copper will begin to bid up the price of copper.

At the same time, if the economic news is that countries such as Germany, France, China, Japan, and the United States are experiencing an economic slowdown or are about to enter a period of slow growth or even a recession, then the price of copper in the market will fall.

Copper in the Consumer Economy

This fact that copper is called Dr. Copper due to its price relationship with the health of the economy can be backed up with the evidence that half of the copper produced goes into electrical components in housing, factories, and offices, as well as in copper pipes. Additionally, since copper is such a good conductor of electricity, it is the primary product in the wiring and lighting of buildings, autos, airplanes, and appliances.

Keep in mind the role of copper in the consumer economy when you observe the price of copper rising and falling with the news. If the U.S. Federal Reserve bank schedules a meeting and reports that the economy is "responding well to the economic easing," or says, "The economy is on course to gain in speed," or any other hints that the U.S. economy is picking up steam and gaining momentum, it is safe to assume that the price of copper will rise in both the near and long term.

If you are reading the news and following economic trends through central banking websites, then cross-check the price of copper in a longer-term chart with your technical analytical software. In this case, using a time frame that gives a one-year price perspective at a minimum of eighteen months or even two years would be better. The idea is that you are trying to gain perspective as to the past pricing of copper in the market.

ESSENTIAL

If the fundamental conditions for copper look good and you are wondering what the charts say, you can use a 200-day/50-day moving average crossover as an indicator to determine how the trade looks "technically." Remember, you are looking for as much evidence as possible that indicate the best time to buy copper.

Even though copper is not used as much as steel and aluminum in construction, its usage in the housing and building industry makes it a better trading opportunity than either of the other two metals. To this evidence, the price of copper will be quoted on CNBC right along with oil, gold, and silver. Rarely will you see steel or aluminum quoted. It is true that steel and aluminum are heavily used in industry, but it is still true that copper's price is easier to predict. Therefore, if you were to go with only one industrial metal in your commodities portfolio, copper would be your best bet.

Building a Basket of Industrial Metals

Remember, you are either going for a basket of commodities in your portfolio or you are going to focus on one or two raw materials to trade. If you are thinking of going the basket route, then you have three choices in which to get into the industrial metals market and therefore gain exposure to the industrial metals: broad-based commodities mutual funds, specialized commodities funds, and company stocks.

The first choice you have is to purchase shares in a broad-based commodities mutual fund. These types of funds contain a mixture of assets that will bring it close to one of the well-known commodities indexes. Many times such funds will have stock of commodities-producing companies as well as ETFs in specific areas of the raw materials spectrum. This means that these funds might have a certain percentage in an ETF that is focused in grains, livestock, or gold. The third element that usually makes up the composition of these mutual funds is a position in futures.

These mutual funds are then comprised of commodities-company stock, commodities ETFs, and commodities futures. Since the mutual funds most likely will be following an index, the percentage composition of the fund will not change much from week to week or from month to month. The stock and ETF portions of the mutual fund's investment portfolio will not change often as it is a more passive style of investing. The third element of the mutual fund's portfolio most likely will consist of commodities futures. The cash balances of the futures accounts of the mutual fund will be "rolled over" on a continuance basis, with the fund manager buying new copper, nickel, and aluminum contracts as the old ones expire. This holding of the main stock and ETF portions, and holding the futures and then rolling over the cash balances, leads to a continuous balance of fully invested funds in the mutual fund.

Specialized Commodities Fund

One thing to consider is that while most fund families offer a general commodities fund, some fund families also will offer a specialized commodities fund, such as a gas and oil fund, or a gold and special minerals fund. If you are looking at different fund families and you haven't yet decided which fund to buy into, you may want to consider this type of fund family.

ALERT

Most of the major fund families such as Oppenheimer, Fidelity, and Vanguard offer these types of general broad-based commodities funds and specialized commodities funds. If you are using a financial advisor, by all means allow her to help you decide which fund family is best for you.

If a firm is offering a specialized commodities mutual fund, you could build a very easy-to-buy and maintain commodities section into your overall portfolio. You may decide to buy a general commodities fund and then accent your commodities exposure with an industrial metals fund as the economic situation begins to improve and therefore lead to a good time to get into the industrial metals.

If you do this, then you could rotate your share balances among funds within the same fund family, usually at no additional fee. You could buy a general commodities fund and a gold and special minerals fund in the same family. Later on, when the economy starts to heat up, you would shift a percentage of the gold fund into an industrial metals fund within the same fund family.

This timing approach is easy to do, and although it triggers a tax consequence (as there would be a sale and therefore gains), it allows you to piggyback not only on the rising price of gold during the first leg of the overall worldwide commodities price increases, but you then can switch into a commodity category that is set to gain in the early-to-mid stages of a commodities upswing in prices. This piggybacking can have the effect of really catapulting your investment account to higher and higher profits as the years go by.

Industrial Metals ETFs and Company Stocks

There are a few other ways to invest in the industrial metals. The first is to invest in an ETF that is specialized to have these metals in its holdings. A good place to start your search for the best industrial metals ETFs is the ETF Database, or ETFdb, website (*http://etfdb.com/type/commodity/industrial-metals*). This site contains all of the ETFs that are in the commodities universe.

Included on the ETFdb site is the "Industrial Metals ETF List." Some of these types of wide-based industrial metals ETFs are called base metals ETFs. In addition to this there are categories for bull and bear leveraged ETFs that are invested in industrial metals. Lastly there are specialized industrial metals ETFs. Examples of these include iPath Pure Beta Aluminum (FOIL), iPath Pure Beta Copper (CUPM), and iPath Pure Beta Nickel (NINI). Although it is not covered in this chapter, there is also an iPath Pure Beta Lead (LEDD).

If you want to build a commodities portfolio that is made up of ETFs but you would like to know where to start as far as percentages of each component, the best thing to do is to compare some of the better-known commodities index's component percentages. This will show you a reasonable percentage amount for each commodity to include in your portfolio.

These ETFs are a great way to get exposure to the industrial metals and to include them in your portfolio. Not only do these ETFs allow you to buy in to the metals in an easy way, these funds also are fully tradable intra-day, meaning you are able to buy and sell them during the day with no restrictions. You will only have to pay transaction costs to buy and then to sell when the commodities have risen in value. This can be really cost effective if you have an online discount broker such as E*TRADE, Scottrade, and TD Ameritrade. These brokers allow for low minimum balances in your account, quick funding through bank transfers, and easy-to-open accounts in addition to very low trading costs.

Clearly these ETFs offer the best of both worlds, as you can get the stability and diversification of a mutual fund. You also get the low transaction costs that are the hallmark of the mutual fund trade. In addition, you will have the tradability of the ETF, with no restrictions, whereas you would not have the ability to buy and sell a commodities mutual fund in a short time frame. Most of these mutual funds are very specialized and therefore smaller in total value. Thus, there are usually heavy restrictions on short-term buying and selling. In other words, you may be charged a 3 percent or higher fee if you sell out of the fund within ninety days of first buying into it. Although it may not seem high, the 3 percent does subtract from the profitability of the trade. In addition to the fee, the fund may restrict your re-buying into the fund within ninety days following the sale of the fund, or even lock you out of the fund entirely. These restrictions are not part of the ETFs. The ETFs are designed to be traded and are heavily traded within the private world of high-net-worth money managers and hedge funds.

Company Stock

Another method of investing in the industrial metals is to invest directly into the companies that mine raw industrial metals or produce finished industrial metals. Since the mines for iron ore, the producers of steel, and the miners of copper, nickel, and aluminum are widely distributed, you would do well to buy in to a company that has mining and manufacturing production in well-diversified countries.

The most complete and accurate listing of companies that can be bought and sold in your brokerage account can be found on the Yahoo! Finance Basic Materials/Metal Mining/Company List website page (*http://biz.yahoo.com/p/_basicm-metals.html*).

CHAPTER 14

The Food Commodities

No commodities investment would be complete without the inclusion of the grains and other foodstuffs into your portfolio. Also known as the *soft commodities*, these are the assets that are related to planting, growing, and harvesting. With this in mind, the foods are a special class of commodities. Their supply and demand functions are a bit more flat than other commodities and are reactionary to growing seasons and weather conditions as well as to the usual inflationary concerns.

Grains, Grub, and Gains

There is another class of commodities that are included in the often-quoted commodities indexes. These are the food commodities, which are composed of coffee, cocoa, sugar, corn, wheat, soybeans, soybean oil, milk, butter, etc. These soft commodities, as they are often called, should be thought of as a special class of commodities.

The reason they are in a special class of commodities is that they are grown and harvested as opposed to mined or drilled for via wells. With this in mind, the thinking is that these grains and crops are, in fact, renewable. Since they have a growing season, and they are planted, cared for, harvested, and then replanted the next season, they are effectively a "renewable resource." This renewable resource factor puts the food commodities into a special class because as long as there are planting seeds left over from the previous year's crop, the planting will go on in the following year and the year after that, and on and on.

So you can see how the price of crops that are used as foodstuffs for both people and animals are not tied to the fact that there is going to be less and less of the commodity in the future. Unlike oil, gasoline, copper, and nickel, there is an idea that the crops of corn, cocoa, and sugar will go on for some time in the future. That "time" may actually be very long as agricultural companies in the United States and in Europe are constantly mixing different forms of crops to get better and better yields (think higher output per acre). These agricultural companies are also devising ways in which the seed for the corn, cocoa, and wheat is heartier and able to grow in harsher soil conditions, and with shorter growing seasons.

FACT

It is true that foods and grains are a renewable resource and are not subject to the eventual "using up" as are some of the other commodities. But it does remain that their price is tied to the volume of dollars that are in the economic system; thus, a key element in their price is inflation.

Add to this the fact that seeds have been made more and more resistant to insect-borne disease, coupled with better and better planting skills such as rotating crops to prevent premature soil erosion and soil nutrient depletion, and you have very abundant growing seasons indeed.

The Food Commodities Market

When there is particularly good market news alluding to the fact that economic times are good and are getting better, the demand side of the foodstuff equation will remain strong. The demand side will be twofold: First is the added inflation that comes during good times. This is natural and is definitely felt in all forms of commodities including foods. Second, there will be an added demand because there will be an increased "appetite" for foodstuffs in general. This increase in appetite will coincide with the overall increase in the wealth of developing nations that often accompanies good times in the developed world. The net effect is an added rise in the demand side of the equation of foodstuffs commodities.

In addition to this demand side, there is the chance of a bad crop, which seems to happen more often than not. Keeping in mind that bad harvests are very difficult to predict, it is best to remember that they will only help the price of your foodstuffs holdings if there happens to be a bad growing season in one of the major food-producing areas or nations. The future for foodstuffs is very difficult to predict, but if played with indirect investments such as foodstuffs companies, ETFs, and mutual funds, you will do well.

Coffee

One of the biggest parts of the food commodities sector is coffee. While coffee futures do not add up in dollars as much as some of the other traded futures, only oil has more physical volume traded than coffee. Coffee is enjoyed all over the world, including Europe and the United States. In fact, in some of the major coffee-consuming nations, coffee is an integral part of the culture.

If you are thinking of getting into trading coffee, you can do so with ETFs or coffee futures. Again, as discussed in other parts of this book, you can purchase an ETF that is especially financially engineered to have its price move up and down right along with the coffee market. A good example of this hard-to-find ETF is the iPath Pure Beta Coffee (CAFE). Adding this unique ETF to your portfolio is one of the easiest ways to gain exposure to this sector of the commodities market.

The other way in which to invest in coffee is through the futures market. The futures market is very difficult to learn, but if you get control of the large amounts of leverage and risk, you will be able to put yourself in a position to gain money when the time comes. Coffee futures are traded at the New York Board of Trade and are subject to all of the risks that go along with trading futures.

FACT

There are two basic types of coffee. The first is Arabica coffee, which has a strong bold taste and aroma. This type of coffee is of the highest quality and is the most difficult to grow. Arabica represents about 60 percent of the coffee market. Robusta is a type of coffee that is of lesser quality and is less expensive to grow.

The final way in which to get into the business of coffee without the ETFs or the futures market is to buy coffee-company stocks or café-company stocks. These would include buying stock in Green Mountain Coffee, a coffee grower; Starbucks; and Caribou Coffee, a coffee-house company with a wilderness theme. More information about the coffee business can be found at the International Coffee Organization (*www.ico.org*) and the National Coffee Association of USA (*www.ncausa.org*).

Cocoa

Another soft commodity, or foodstuffs commodity, is cocoa. The consumption of cocoa started in Central America and South America. Early European explorers liked the taste of cocoa and brought the plants home for cultivation in Africa, which the settlers were beginning to colonize. Today most of the world's cocoa is made and grown in Africa, including the Ivory Coast and Ghana. In addition to Africa, a large percentage of the world's cocoa crop is grown in Indonesia.

As with all of the food commodities, knowing when to invest and trade in them is very tricky. In order to capture the price movement of a product like cocoa, you have to follow the information trail, just as if you were investing in any other commodity.

ALERT

Cocoa is a cash crop of many countries. This means that these countries have a large part of their entire export in one product: in this case, cocoa. When these countries have a bad growing season, or when there is news of bad weather, the price of cocoa in the world's market will rise rapidly.

With this said, the World Cocoa Foundation (WCF)'s website (*www .worldcocoafoundation.org*) can be a good place to look for any indication that the time is right to buy in to this crop. Since cocoa is a crop that is traded worldwide but produced by farms that are very distant from the United States, it may be best to buy into an ETF such as the iPath Pure Beta Cocoa (CHOC). This ETF would offer a very cost-effective and easy-to-manage way to gain exposure to this part of the commodities arena. There are cocoa futures that are traded at the CME Group in Chicago (*www .cmegroup.com/trading/agricultural/softs/cocoa.html*).

Another thing to consider is that cocoa is grown in parts of the world that may have labor problems. While cocoa has the usual growing-season problems such as bad seasons and failed crops, there is the added element of labor strikes on the farms and in the processing plants themselves.

A strike such as this caused the prices of cocoa to spike rapidly in the early spring of 2012. If you were on the long side of the trade (meaning you would make money when the price of cocoa went up) you would have done well, and for sure, many futures traders made their money for the month very quickly. On the other hand, if you were on the short end of the trade, meaning you would have made money if the price of cocoa were to go down, you would have been caught on the wrong side and would have lost money quickly. Again, this represents the difficulty in predicting the prices of some soft commodities.

Sugar

Sugar is also a foodstuff that can be included in your commodities portfolio. Sugar is produced all over the world, but the main producers are in Brazil and India, with the United States following in third place. Like the other food commodities, sugar is a renewable resource as it is grown and harvested each and every growing season.

With this in mind, it too is subject to the slower, steadier gains in price that are related more to the overall inflation rate than to increased demand. While it is true that more sugar will be sold when the economies of the world are doing well (mainly due to the flow-down effect of the increased wealth in the developed countries to the developing countries), there will be more of a price effect due to inflation. This inflationary effect will be the main price driver for sugar. This is true because the sugar industry and the world's demand for sugar are very stable and therefore very constant.

FACT

While sugar is normally a slower, steadier trade, the sugar ETFs were up nearly 10 percent in the first quarter of 2012! Just as with all commodities, there can be a surge in prices that are driven up by the world's traders as well as by supply and demand. This can cause prices of foodstuffs to rise very rapidly!

There is only so much sugar that will be consumed by the world's population year after year. This is true even if there were a great increase in the overall wealth of the world. The demand of sugar will go up incrementally as the developing nations became wealthier with time. With this in mind, the short-term price of sugar can be very difficult to predict, and therefore difficult to trade on a short-term basis.

If you wanted to add to your commodities portfolio and add sugar to your holdings, you would be best served by either sugar futures or a specialized commodity ETF invested in sugar. As far as the sugar futures go, there are two contracts available for you to trade. The first is called Sugar No. 11. This sugar futures contract has its price based on the overall price of "world sugar." At the same time there is a second sugar futures contract that is traded at the New York Mercantile Exchange (NYMEX) called Sugar No. 14. This contract has its price based on sugar that is produced in the United States only.

Of course, you could trade a sugar ETF such as the iPath Pure Beta Sugar (SGAR). This ETF would give you exposure to the sugar market in a very easy manner.

Corn and Wheat

Corn is the most widely produced food product. Its main producers are the Breadbasket (Great Plains region) of the United States, followed by China, Brazil, and then Mexico. Corn is used as a food for both people and livestock and also used increasingly as ethanol in the United States, which is added to gasoline and fuels. In fact, this addition of corn-based alcohol has been the cause of an additional factor in the recent increase in the price of corn prices worldwide. While having the effect of keeping gasoline cheaper at the pump and offering economic relief to consumers that are drivers, it has caused an economic strain on livestock farmers who rely on corn for feed, as well as the everyday consumer of corn as staple food. In fact there was controversy in October 2010, when the U.S. government allowed the level of ethanol content in gasoline to be increased from the previous maximum level of 10 percent to a new maximum level of 15 percent. In this manner, adding corn to your trading account can round out a commodities portfolio that otherwise would be invested only in oil, precious metals, and industrial metals.

There are three ways to invest in corn. The first and most aggressive way is to buy corn futures. These futures are heavily traded by corn farmers as a hedging technique against the cash crop of corn. Because of this, there will be a greater number of corn contracts at the onset of the growing season.

The second method of buying corn futures is with the same type of specialized commodity ETF that would be invested in only corn. A good example of this type of ETF is the Teucrium Corn Fund (NYSE: CORN).

The last way to gain exposure in the corn market is to buy a company that specializes in growing corn (among other grains) and in the production of foods. A good example of this type of company is Archer Daniels Midland Company (ADM) (*www.adm.com*).

ESSENTIAL

An investment in a food company such as Archer Daniels Midland (ADM) can serve many purposes. It can get you into the commodities world and into the grains and foodstuffs without difficult trading. At the same time, the stock pays a dividend with a 2.25 percent yield annually!

Wheat

Wheat is an agricultural commodity that is produced in numbers second only to corn. The production of wheat is led by China, India, and the United States. Wheat futures are traded on the Chicago Board of Trade (CBOT). (Each contract of wheat on the Chicago Board of Trade represents 5,000 bushels of #2 Soft Red Winter Wheat or for a 3-cent premium per bushel, #1 Soft Red Winter Wheat.) They can be traded in an electronic manner with a futures trading account; its symbol is ZW.

There is also a mini-wheat contract. Since this contract has a smaller size of 1,000 bushels, it's easier to trade for those with smaller futures accounts. As with other mini contracts, there are a large number of people who prefer this size. Futures contracts that are 1/5 or 1/10 the physical unit size of the norm are called *minis*. Don't be fooled by the term mini! There is much money to be made with these smaller contracts. For example, a commodity trading house might enter into one of these mini-wheat futures as a way to test a new trading technique. Of course, they could use the smaller contacts to build a hedge for one of their smaller clients who is a small to mid-sized wheat farmer.

Again, a commodities portfolio would not be complete without a representation of the soft commodities. When thinking of building a position, keep in mind that 9.5 percent of one entire well-known commodities index, the Rogers Commodity Index *www.rogersrawmaterials.com* is composed of only these two, corn and wheat!

Again, an investment in ADM (*www.adm.com*) would give you a conservative exposure to the food industry and the food commodities market and at the same time be more traditional in nature.

Soybeans: Food and Fuel

Soybeans as a subgroup represent a food that is widely used by both people and livestock. Soy can be traded as beans, soybean oil, and soybean meal. The number-one producer of soybeans is the United States. The soybean crop is subject to bad growing seasons, as are the other crops. These good crop/bad crop years can add to the volatility of the price of soybeans and soybean products.

In addition, many fuel producers in the United States and Europe are adding soybean oil to regular diesel fuel to create a hybrid biodiesel. With oil prices on the rise, there will certainly be more widespread use of soybean oil in the manufacture of biodiesel. As it becomes more popular and proven in use, it will create an upward demand in soybeans and soybean oil that will last for years to come. As with the ethanol in gasoline, the added use of soybean products as an additive to diesel fuel will have a mixed effect. It will keep the price of this fuel down at the pump, which will financially help those who rely on diesel for their vehicles. At the same time, it will cause increased demand of the grain, which will then cause the price of soybean products to rise in price for those who use it as a foodstuff.

Like wheat, there is a mini-soybeans contract that is traded at the CME in Chicago. You would be able to trade one of these contracts electronically with an online futures account. As with the mini-wheat contract, the mini-soybeans contract is for 1,000 bushels, as opposed to the full sized contract of 5,000 bushels. Again, these mini contracts are good for the smaller and average sized futures account. They are also good for getting started in futures trading as their up and down swings in prices are smaller due to the smaller bushel size of each contract.

All types of soy product futures are traded at the Chicago Board of Trade. Again, an investment in a food company such as Archer Daniels Midland (*www.adm.com*) would be a conservative play in the food industry and grain-growing business.

To sum up, all well-thought-out commodities investment portfolios should include a bit of the soft commodities. If you are going for a more complex trading portfolio, you can go for the futures in the grains, cocoa, or sugar. If you want a more conservative portfolio, you would be well served with a specialized ETF or even a grain-related commodity company.

CHAPTER 15

How to Invest in Physical Commodities

This chapter will teach you the basics of buying commodities that you can actually hold in your hand. While some may enjoy trading commodities electronically, you may find it more to your liking that you go through the process of paying cash for goods received. In this case, the goods are gold and silver bars and coins. You may find that this classic form of money, physical precious metals, fits perfectly in your commodity investment plans.

Actually Owning It for Peace of Mind

One of the most satisfying ways to invest in raw materials is through buying and owning the actual physical commodity itself. While this is impractical with most of the commodities, such as corn, steel, and cocoa, it is very possible with the buying and owning of gold, silver, and platinum coins and bars.

If you are considering buying gold or silver for your commodities investment, you should think of the security of having the actual metals on hand. While you would have to buy a futures fund, ETF, or mutual fund to own most of the commodities, it can be quite easy to find precious metals or coin dealers or jewelers in your area (or on the Internet). You can then go to these dealers to buy a variety of actual gold and silver in metal form. Unlike other investments, once you own a gold coin or silver bar, the investment is yours to keep, and you may find that the added bonus of holding your investment in your hand goes a long way toward giving you the feeling of peace of mind in the added safety of your investment.

Some say owning the precious metals that were once **monetized** (meaning they were once used for actual money) is the best way of investing in commodities. While this may be true, it can be then said that the best way to own gold and silver is to take actual physical delivery of the metals.

Unlike a paper contract such as a futures contract or ETF, actual gold and silver metal is the surest way of keeping your investment safe. You can pay for the coins, take them with you, and then put them in a secure location in your home or put them in a safe-deposit box in a bank.

ALERT

If you are collecting silver and gold bars and coins, then you need to think about where you will be storing them. These metals are costly; it might be worth investing in a heavy home safe with a good lock on it. Also, never speak of this gold and silver to strangers: keep it quiet, and keep it private!

When you pay for your gold and silver you can then feel the heft and weight of the metals as you hold them in your hands. You can build a collection of common, yet very interesting old European gold coins from the late nineteenth and early twentieth centuries. You may find it to be your thing to buy as many different gold coins as you can, with the only prerequisite that they have a high gold content and a low premium. (Gold and silver dealers usually charge a percentage over the price of the actual gold content of the coin; this is how they make money.)

You also may want to buy silver in as many different shapes and sizes as you can find. If you are like most people, you will find that half of the fun of investing is in buying the investment. With this in mind, you can make weekly runs to your favorite coin dealer to see what silver you can buy "on the cheap." You might discover that you like to buy circulated U.S. Morgan silver dollars (which are 0.77343 ounces of pure silver each). Or you might discover that you want to build a collection of common date U.S. Barber, Standing Liberty, and Washington 90 percent silver quarters. On the other hand, you may prefer the weight and feel of a 10-ounce bar of pure silver that is 0.999+ fine. These "open palm" sized bars can be quite impressive (and costly!), but they offer a very stout and condensed form of wealth that is well suited for a home safe of bank safe-deposit box. This chapter will get you into the basics of buying and selling the precious metals commodities through your local coin dealer, jeweler, or over the Internet.

The Basics of Physical Investing and Trading

The basics of physical gold and silver investing include three things: fineness (pureness of the metal), weight, and premium. These are the key elements in determining the value of a coin or bar that you consider buying from a coin or precious metals dealer.

- **Fineness.** A number in 1000ths that defines the purity of the gold or silver in a coin or bar. Example: a pre-1964 U.S. quarter is 0.900 fine, or 90 percent silver and 10 percent nonprecious metal.

- **Weight.** Coins and bars will have the weight of the pure gold content or pure silver content measured to four decimal places of an ounce. The actual pure content is called actual gold weight (AGW) or actual silver weight (ASW).
- **Premium.** All dealers price their gold and silver by taking the market price as quoted on the Internet (called the ***spot price***) and adding to it a small percentage called a ***premium***.

As with jewelry, there is a certain karat or purity to gold coins and bars. There is also the fact that sterling silver must be 0.925 pure in order to be considered sterling grade. Most gold coins and bars are made as an ***alloy***. This means that they are manufactured with one or more other metals besides the pure gold and silver. Metals used in the alloy manufacturing process include copper and bronze, which are included in the gold and silver coins and bars to give them added hardness and strength, and to make them more resistant to corrosion.

FACT

Paying high premiums on gold and silver coins can eat into your profits. Keep in mind that rare, small coins or bars have higher percentage premiums, as do numismatic, or collector, coins. It is also true that the "uglier" or more "industrial" the form of the metal bar or coin, the lower the percentage of the premium.

With this in mind, when you are comparing one gold coin to another, you must consider not just the weight and size of the coin or bar. It may be that the coin you want to buy is actually 0.900 fine, meaning that it is 90 percent gold and 10 percent other metal, such as copper or silver. If the coin is this composition, it is most likely a European coin. On the other hand, if the coin is British, Canadian, or Australian, the coin is most likely 0.9166 fine, which equates to 22 karats.

Most of these 22-karat fine coins are quite old and come from a time when gold was used as a form of monetary exchange. On the other hand, many of today's gold coins are 0.999 or even 0.9999 fine, which equates to 24-karat, also known as ***pure gold***.

To explain it further, when you go to a coin dealer and ask for a 1-ounce gold coin, the dealer might show you an American Gold Eagle and a Canadian Maple Leaf. The American Gold Eagle is 0.917 fine gold. This means that the other 0.083 is made up of different metals for wear purposes to equal 1.000, or 100 percent, of the coin. In the American Gold Eagle, the 0.083 part is made of copper and silver. Even though this coin is not pure gold, it still contains exactly 1-ounce of pure gold in actual gold weight (AGW), after the copper and silver is calculated in to the alloy.

Gold Is Gold!

The Canadian Maple Leaf, on the other hand, is 0.9999 fine, or 24 karats. This coin too will contain exactly 1-ounce of pure gold in actual gold weight. The difference is that the Canadian Maple Leaf is purer, but this does not make a difference in the total gold content of the coin: Both are 1-ounce gold coins in actual gold weight. The 24-karat purity of the Maple Leaf does not add to its value in any way: Gold is gold! In fact, most dealers will charge less for a 0.9999 fine 24-karat gold Canadian Maple Leaf and more for the "less pure" 0.917 fine American Gold Eagle! This is true because the American Gold Eagles are very popular in the United States, while gold coins from foreign countries are not as popular. This means that foreign coins are slower to sell and move out of the dealer's inventory, and thus dealers have more of them in stock. Hint: Foreign coins are good buys to be had!

What is called fractional gold is another good buy. ***Fractional gold*** is what is commonly referred to as the older European and Asian gold coins. These coins usually came in 0.900 fine gold, but in odd sizes that were tied into the exchange rates of the issuing countries. Remember, most of these coins were issued at a time when gold was still being used as money and to pay bills, even if at the national level. With this in mind, there are many European coins that have unusual amounts of AGW, such as the 0.1867 ounces AGW of the Swiss, French, and Belgian 20 Francs; the 0.1947 ounces

AGW of the 0.900 fine Netherlands 10 guilders; and the 0.2354 ounces AGW in British Sovereigns.

When you are considering these coins, remember, you are buying the weight of the gold plus paying a small premium. With this in mind, oftentimes it can be much cheaper to buy a vintage French Rooster 20 Franc (per fractional ounce of gold) than it would be to buy the same amount of gold per ounce in a newly issued American Gold Eagle. This is true because dealers often sell fractional, old gold at a much lower premium than the new American Gold Eagle counterparts. For example, the premium on a ¼-ounce American Gold Eagle can be 12–15 percent more than the spot price of the AGW, while a French, Belgian, or Swiss coin can be as little as 6 percent over the spot price of the AGW of the coin. If you shop around, you may find premiums even lower on the Dutch gold coins—the Netherlands 10 guilders—with their unusual actual gold weight of 0.1947 ounces.

ESSENTIAL

Having a good relationship with your gold dealer is key to keeping your gold costs down. You should be able to call your dealer and ask: "I'm looking for cheap gold. Do you have anything you want to sell to me as cheap as possible?" Dealers like to have buyers for odd and hard-to-sell gold denominations and coins, thus charging smaller premiums.

Calculating the Price

How do you calculate the price of a gold or silver coin? First, know the actual gold weight (AGW) of the coin. If it is a Great Britain Sovereign, you know that the AGW is 0.2354 of pure gold. Next, look up the price of spot gold on a website that lists gold prices such as Kitco (*www.kitco.com*). Multiply the spot price of gold listed (it will be quoted in a 1-ounce listing) by the AGW (in ounces) of the coin (in this case, 0.2354.) The result will be the value of the pure gold in the coin (even though the British Gold Sovereign is only 22-karat and not 24-karat pure). Knowing this amount, you can then ask the dealer what his premium is on the Sovereign in percentage terms.

Multiply the AGW value of the coin by the premium to arrive at a fair price for the coin. For example, if the spot price for gold on Kitco is $1,800 per ounce and the dealer has an 8 percent premium on fractional gold, a British Sovereign Gold coin would be calculated as follows:

$1,800 × 0.2354 = $423.72 Value of gold in the British Sovereign

$423.72 × 1.08 = $457.62 Dealer's price of the gold coin with the 8% premium

The same formula holds true for all gold and silver coins and bars.

Investment-Grade Bars

Furthering the idea of buying U.S. and foreign gold and silver coins, you could also buy investment-grade gold and silver bars. The main difference between gold and silver coins and gold and silver bars usually is that bars are a higher-grade fineness (purity) than most coins, and bars are usually larger sized. Coins usually come in 1-ounce, ½-ounce, ¼-ounce, and $\frac{1}{10}$-ounce weights as well as the odd-sized fractional foreign coins made by most any manufacturer or country of origin.

On the other hand, investment-grade bars must carry the hallmark of refiners that are recognized by the world's electronic exchanges. These gold and silver bars are called ***good delivery bars*** because they are certified to be used to satisfy a delivery on a gold or silver futures contract. In addition to specific manufacture of these bars, they must be of a certain fineness, usually 0.995+ fine or greater. The sizes of the bars can range from 5 grams to 400 ounces for gold, and from 1 ounce to 1,000 ounces for silver.

These investment-grade gold and silver bars are of the same types that are included in the warehouse holdings of the world's commodities exchanges. They are also the type that are held at some of the most popular gold and silver trading vehicles: the ETFs such as the popular GLD and SLV and other large-scale gold and silver ETFs storage facilities.

Investment-grade bars can add an additional layer of protection to your physical gold holdings. This is true because these bars are in greater demand when gold and silver prices are rising, creating greater need for gold in the ETFs and storerooms of the futures exchange warehouses. When gold goes up really high in price, there are more and more open contracts in the futures trading, and these must be backed up by increased physical holdings.

FACT

You will find 5-, 10-, and 20-gram 0.999+ gold bars to be the cheapest way to buy gold at most coin and gold dealers. On the other hand, these bars are often sold with the highest premiums on auction websites such as eBay. In both cases it is because these investment-grade gold bars are unusual and thus are hard to find and sell.

Aside from this additional demand, there might come a time in the future when there is the ability to *borrow* against physical gold and silver holdings. In this case, the loans granted would be collateralized by the investment-grade gold bars. The banking industry is evolving continuously, and new banking products are being invented all the time. It is conceivable that term loans would be granted against collateral with a market value that is outside the realm of normal collateral, such as car titles, real estate, or equities. If the market for gold and silver gets really heated up, there is a chance that lenders would take delivery of physical gold and silver, inventory it, value it, place it in vaults, and grant a term loan against the metal deposit.

In this way, it would act as a collateralized margin account, with the collateral being the gold or silver. As with everything, a deposit of investment-grade gold or silver bars would be more readily accepted by the lending institution because the demand in the international trading community would be heightened for the investment-grade gold.

FACT

The USA's vaults at Fort Knox hold approximately 147.3 million ounces of gold. This gold is held at a "book value" of $42.22 per ounce on a permanent basis! This means that the value of the gold held in the vaults has an unrealized capital gain of more than $251 billion!

The preference for investment-grade bars sounds strange, since gold is gold, right? The answer is that it has to do with the "good delivery" of the bars, since the bars with those specific makers' marks would be available to be used to satisfy a futures contract, and they would be in higher demand in a hyper-gold market. Investment-grade bars would be much like any other investment; you can get a margin loan on equities, but you might stand a chance of getting a lower margin loan rate as the quality of the equities got higher.

Pennies

There is also a very interesting and affordable way to "load up" on physical commodities by adding to your stockpile of the industrial metal copper. Although copper is not a precious metal, its price goes up and down in a very volatile nature, much like the price of silver. This means that when the price of gold is moving up and down 1–3 percent per day, the price of silver will move an accelerated rate of 3–5 percent per day. Copper prices will move similarly to those of silver, as both copper and silver are tied to industrial demand.

In other words, if the news is reporting that the economies of the United States, Europe, and Asia are doing well, or are having greater growth than expected, the price of copper will react very positively to this news. This is because copper is one of the core ingredients in building and manufacturing. Thus, it is considered to be an indicator of the industrial world economy; its price can accurately predict good and bad times.

With this being the case, there is a good argument made to have copper in your commodities portfolio. If you are thinking that you would like to go the physical commodities route, then there is a very simple and affordable solution to adding physical copper to your commodities portfolio.

This method involves the buying, sorting, and storage of U.S. pennies. It may be news to you, but the U.S. one-cent pennies that are made today contain almost no copper: They are 97.5 percent zinc that is plated with copper. However, U.S. pennies made in 1982 and earlier are made of 95 percent pure copper and 5 percent zinc. With this in mind, you can go to your bank and buy $25 boxes of pennies for $25 in paper money. Then at home you set up two small containers, and as you open up each roll of pennies, you separate the 1982 and older ones from the 1983 and newer ones.

This process yields about 600 to 700 1982 and older copper pennies per $25 box of pennies. Running the numbers further, you will yield an average of $6.50 in copper pennies and approximately $18.50 in common-date pennies.

In order to fully analyze your yield per $25 box of copper pennies, visit the Coinflation website (*www.coinflation.com*), where the metal value of coins is given. Coinflation publishes a live website with a matrix that factors in the weight of U.S. coins and their metal content. It then uses live market feeds to calculate the actual metal value of each coin.

Going to this site can yield surprises. With copper valued at $3.80 a pound and zinc valued at 92 cents a pound at this writing, the Coinflation site calculates the actual metal value of the copper in a penny dated 1982 to be worth 2.5 cents at this writing.

How can a penny be worth 2½ cents? The answer is that the penny contains 0.006856 pound of copper and that copper has a market value of $3.80 a pound.

Strange, indeed! When the world is moving along fine and the industrial demand for copper is heating up, the price of copper can easily move up to $4 or $4.75 per pound or even higher. The weight of the 95 percent copper in 1982 and older U.S. pennies stays at the same 0.006856 pound of copper in each penny. The difference, however, is that the actual metal value of the penny can jump to 3 cents, 3¾ cents, or even higher with the rising copper prices.

You might think, "Well, this is all good, copper moves in price like gold, oil, and cocoa." But wait! The pennies that are worth 2½, 3, 3½, or more cents apiece never cost more than the price of its face value of 1 cent!

Look at it again: You spend $25 on a box of pennies at the bank. While watching your favorite TV show you spend time sorting through the rolls of coins. Say you sort out $7 in 1982 and older 95 percent copper pennies and $18 in regular, newer pennies, and copper is valued at $3.80 a pound.

Here is the gain:

$7 in 1982 and older pennies = 700 pennies × 2.5 cents each = $17.50 worth of copper

$18 in 1983 and newer pennies = 1,800 pennies × 1 cent each = $18 worth of pennies (which are money!)

Total average yield on $25 face value box of pennies @ $3.80/pound copper = $17.50 + $18 = $35.50

$35.50 − the $25 box of pennies "bought" = a net increase of $10.50 in value!

If you did this you would return the $18 in pennies to the bank and use it toward buying another $25 box of pennies. You would then go about sorting pennies out again, which would yield another 600 to 700 of the 95 percent copper pennies.

QUESTION

How much can I make sorting through a $25 box of pennies?
When copper is $4.25 per pound, you will earn an average of $25 per hour by sorting through the pennies in a $25 box. The higher the price of copper, the more you will make in gains per coin, but the number of 1982 and older 95 percent copper coins remains the same.

Keep in mind that these lower prices of copper in the market at this writing are due to the slower economy as a result of the economic crisis of 2008; prices should be rising again. Your hoard of copper pennies could be stored in large containers in a basement or attic, and be accumulated over time.

This method offers a very affordable way in which to invest in the industrial metal copper, with the only issue being the time it takes to sort through the coins and then later to sell them. You may find that this is an acceptable way to compromise on an addition to your commodities portfolio: You may find that the money you are spending on the premiums in silver and gold are offset with the money that is being saved by the added value of sorting through copper coins in your own time. The net effect is that you will find you have tens and tens (or hundreds and hundreds if you like this method) of pounds of copper in your basement or other storage area.

The next question is what to do with the copper once it is sorted and separated into the 95 percent copper penny category. The answer is simple: Hold the copper coins until there is an adequate rise in the price of copper, and then sell them on a website such as eBay. These copper pennies are being sold on eBay now, even at the price of only 2½ cents per penny. This is because copper is a commodity just like any other, and there are people who recognize the fact that accumulating the 1982 and older 95 percent copper pennies is an excellent way to load up on the industrial metal as an investment. These people cruise the Internet looking for opportunities to buy copper because they know that copper will rise in price in the coming years. They know that by buying the older copper pennies they are buying 95 percent pure physical copper. This copper is just as good as a copper ingot, and in many ways is not much different in theory than a 95 percent pure gold of silver bar. They are all physical commodities with active trading markets. *There is money to be made in copper pennies!*

CHAPTER 16

Scrap Gold and Junk Silver

If you find that you like buying physical gold and silver from a coin dealer, then you might enjoy going the other route, and buying scrap gold and junk silver. Hunting for scrap gold and junk silver can take a bit of training to know how to do it effectively. Once you know how the basics of karat, weights, and melt price per gram, you will be well on your way to getting into the business of shopping for and buying gold and silver "on the cheap."

Buying Metals "On the Cheap"

There is another way to enjoy shopping for and buying gold and silver. In this alternate method, you take your treasure hunting skills to the max and go to antique shops, secondhand stores, and vintage jewelry stores in search of vintage and old gold and silver jewelry. In addition to the gold and silver jewelry that can be found at these stores, there is also the likely chance that you'll find silver flatware as well as silver serving trays, salt shakers, and so on. As with shopping for coins and bars at a coin dealer, you will be buying for weight, fineness, and, sometimes, design.

This is the way professional gold dealers fill out their coffers of gold and silver. You too can make the rounds with weekly or semiweekly trips to your neighborhood antique stores (or online, as discussed later in this chapter) and scout out 10-karat, 14-karat, and 18-karat gold and sterling-silver jewelry and housewares. Believe it or not, the chance of going into a secondhand clothing store, antique shop, or antique mall to look for and actually find high-quality gold and silver items is very high. It is quite easy to find vintage rings and other jewelry that are "out of style" and are made from perfectly good 10- and 14-karat gold that are selling *below their melt value*!

ALERT

You need to learn to get a feel for the actual gold weight in rings and jewelry that have jewelry stones in them. It is still possible to make money by buying used gold rings and then selling them for scrap. The key is to get to know by sight how much 14-karat gold weighs by its volume.

The idea is that you would go into an antique mall and scout for gold and silver items. The next step is to evaluate the karat (the fineness of the gold) and discreetly evaluate the value of that gold content using your best estimate of the actual gold weight (AGW). From there it is easy to calculate the melt value of the item; you can then make a bid to buy the item at or below its AGW value.

Gold items are easier to find than silver items. It seems that professional antique buyers are enamored with vintage silver candlesticks, salt shakers, and flatware. You will most likely find that the "premium" added to buying the silver weight of the sterling-silver item prohibits the buying of the fork, spoon, serving tray, etc., for its weight value. In other words, these items are usually valued well above their "intrinsic value," meaning that the value of the item rests mainly in collector and historical value beyond the lump of silver that it is made of.

The same is usually *not* true for gold. You will find plenty of old wedding bands, old stickpins, ugly men's signet rings, and other jewelry that is made of perfectly fine 10-karat and 14-karat gold.

Gold Fineness, Karat, and Markings

Just as you must when you are planning to purchase gold coins and bars from a coin dealer, you must consider the fineness and weight of the gold object before you buy it. The best and easiest way to do this is to *only* buy gold items that are clearly marketed by their karat value. With this method, you will be insuring that the vintage and gold items you are buying have the gold content that you are pricing the item at. For example, you may find older gold with unusual fineness, such as 9-karat or 10-karat in addition to the usual 14-karat and 18-karat. These finenesses will be clearly marked somewhere on the gold item.

You might find it helpful to carry with you a *loupe*, or jewelry magnifying glass, on your shopping trips; one with 10×–30× power works the best. Also, when buying a loupe, think of investing in the best that you can afford, as optics cost money: You will find that a few dollars more will go a long way toward better quality.

Knowing the Melt Value

The process of buying gold for weight is the process of knowing the melt value of the jewelry. For example, you decide to make your weekly trip to an antique mall near your home. You know it is a good time to go because gold has been increasing in value for the past week or two, and now is up 1 percent for the day. Before you leave for the antique mall, you go online to one of the best gold and silver price quote sites on the Internet, Kitco.com (*www.kitco.com*). You note that the price of the gold is at $1,739 per ounce.

ESSENTIAL

You can build technology into the lost art of gold dealing. One of the best ways to do this is to carry a Smartphone with an Internet hookup. You would then take this phone (or tablet computer such as an iPad or similar) and call Kitco to get up-to-the-second "live pricing" just like online trading!

Next, you move to the part of the website that says "Buy Silver/Gold." You then go to the part that says "Unrecognized Bars." From there, you notice that Kitco is listing the "melt sales price" of gold in karats. In other words, you can look up "9 karat" and you will see that at a gold price of $1,739 per ounce (for an ounce of 24-karat gold), 1 *gram* of 9-karat gold would be worth $19.51. (Note the difference in the unit from *ounce* to *gram*: 1 ounce = 28.3495231 grams.)

In the same manner, 1 gram of 10-karat gold would be worth (at melt) $21.71. One gram of 14-karat gold would be worth $30.48 (of AGW) and 18-karat would be worth $39.57 per gram. Keep in mind that a site like Kitco automatically calculates the actual gold weight of the 9-, 10-, 14-, 18-, 22-, and 24-karat gold, and calculates the value of that AGW per gram at that gold price. These prices are live and change with the up and down price movement of the gold (or silver, or platinum, if that is what you are buying).

Estimating Gold Weight by Karat

If you want to look at it longhand, you would find the gram weight of the gold, and then multiply it by the price of the gold per gram, and then multiply that by the fineness of the gold.

With this in mind, a quick rule of thumb when you are on site in an antique shop is to look up the price of the gold per ounce, divide by 32.15 to arrive at the number of grams (as there are approximately 32.15 grams in 1 Troy ounce, different from normal ounces), and then multiply by the following according to the fineness of the gold (this can easily be done with the calculator function on a Smartphone):

Fineness	
9 karat	0.375 Pure Gold per Gram
10 karat	0.417 Pure Gold per Gram
12 karat	0.500 Pure Gold per Gram
14 karat	0.583 Pure Gold per Gram
18 karat	0.750 Pure Gold per Gram
22 karat	0.917 Pure Gold per Gram
24 karat	0.999+ Pure Gold per Gram

When you are looking for the fineness markings of the gold jewelry, you may notice that instead of the karat marking there is the numerical value of the gold. This is often the case of very old gold, or gold that is not made in the United States. You may find a broach that is German, Austrian, or other European make, for example, and upon close inspection with your loupe you may notice a ".750," ".500," or ".417" on the piece. These markings indicate the fineness, or percentage of metal purity, of the gold without the "karat" markings. If you find such a piece of vintage jewelry and it is not priced as gold (because it was not known to be gold due to the fact that the "karat" mark was not clearly visible), you can then make estimates as to the weight of the gold.

Estimating the weight of the gold in the object can be easy if you get the knack of it. When you first start learning the weight of gold objects, you could easily find an accurate weight by using a jewelry scale. Jewelry scales can be bought online, through eBay, at coin dealers, and at hobby stores. These digital scales are very accurate and can be set to measure down to the tenth of a gram.

FACT

Even the best digital jewelry scales are affordable when you buy them online. You can do an Internet search for "digital scale" or buy one on a website like eBay. The suppliers will offer several different types; it is best to get one that is small and fits in a shirt pocket or purse.

In order to use the scale to best advantage, you would take the object, such as a thick 14-karat gold wedding band, set the scale to zero, and gently place the ring on the small metal contact pad of the scale. A wide 14-karat wedding band will weigh about 3.8 grams, give or take a tenth of a gram. Once you have the weight of the wedding band as told from the digital readout on the scale and you have confirmed with your loupe that it is a certain karat of gold, then you quickly check against the prices of melt gold per gram values according to its karat.

This takes a quick bit of math on the calculator of your Smartphone: Take the grams of the gold times the value of that karat gold at today's prices. This equals the "melt value" of the gold and is very close to the amount of money that the object would realize if sold for scrap. While it is not always suggested that items be scrapped, it would be very common to collect vintage and older out-of-date jewelry over time, separately bagging each piece with its weight, karat, and the price paid for it. The value of gold is high: a few rings, necklaces, and pocket watches (or other collection that you've gathered over the months and years) can add up to a lot of gold in AGW, which can lead to big dollar amounts.

Sterling Silver, from Kitchen to Safe

Sterling silver is silver that is used in flatware, salt and pepper shakers, and trays. If not polished, sterling items will have a bluish or even blackened appearance. In addition to this coloration, sterling will be noticeably heavier than a regular stainless item. This is because silver is much denser than stainless. **Sterling silver** is an alloy that contains 92.5 percent silver—0.925 fine—and 7.5 percent other metals, usually copper. When an object is referred to as being *sterling silver* it means that it meets the minimum alloy of .925 pure silver.

When looking for sterling, look for old patterns that are "out of style" or old sets of flatware that are organized in plastic bags or even the original wood cases. Check to make sure that the pieces are in fact marked "Sterling" or ".925" or "925." These are the markings that you should be looking for to determine whether something is made of sterling silver. A marking such as "Plate," "Silver Plate," "Silver over Stainless" means that the item is silver plated. While silver-plated items may have collectible value, they usually do not contain enough silver value for "melt value."

ALERT

If you really like hunting for and buying gold and silver items at secondhand stores and antique shops, you may begin to find that your collection of gold and silver grows. Shop around for the best prices on bank safe-deposit boxes; oftentimes a box that is larger will be the best value.

On a side note, there is a whole market for silver items that fall under the area of collector items. Most of these items are older in nature and very fancy. Some of them are worth collecting on this merit alone, which precludes the notion that you are buying them based on their silver weight only (in fact, vintage silver dealers would consider this notion of buying by weight utterly ridiculous!) If you think you would like to get into buying vintage and antique silver for collectible value, you can still use the scales to determine the silver content of the item.

Weighing Sterling Items

The best way to weigh your silver items is to place a cardboard box big enough to hold the loose silver items on the metal measuring pad of the scale (these metal pads are usually only 2–3 inches square or less.) After the cardboard box is placed on the scale, turn on the scale. The scale will then "tare" to the weight of the box, and will set to zero. When a scale "tares," it sets its zero amounts to include the item first placed on it, and then it will record in grams any additional weight that is placed in the box, *not including the weight of the box*. In other words, you may find that you have bought a set of sterling flatware that services twelve. You know that the set was a very good deal, and since it was marked "925", you decide to see the weight of one place setting.

The first thing you should do is to obtain a small box. The small red coin file boxes work well for this task, as would any other box that is just big enough to hold a place setting. Place the box on the jewelry scale, wait a few seconds, and then press the "on" button of the scale. The scale will then "tare" and set to zero.

The next step would be to place a salad fork, dinner fork, and one of each of the spoons in the place setting in the box gently. Do not add the knife, as this is treated separately. After gently putting the items of the place setting in the box, wait for the scale to read out the weight in grams and tenths. Write this number down.

The next step is to measure the weight of the knife of the place setting. Remove the previously measured items and set them aside. Turn the scale off and replace the empty box on the scale. Turn the scale on and wait for the scale to tare to the box. Gently place one knife in the box, and wait for the scale to measure in grams. The next step is special for the knife: Since most knives will have a stainless-steel blade, only 10 percent of the measured gram weight should be recorded as sterling weight. In other words, if the knife weighs 64 grams, only 6.4 grams (10 percent) is to be considered sterling silver weight.

Do the same procedure for all of the serving items, such as a gravy ladle, in the set, and add them up. You will then determine an average sterling weight per place setting, which is then multiplied by the number of place settings per set. This number is added to the weights of the additional side pieces. The same could be done for any other sterling sets of salt shakers, candlestick holders, or other items that you may find.

ESSENTIAL

Keep in mind that the sterling silver items you find may be worth much more than the price of their sterling content alone. Some patterns in the sterling pieces are very collectible as antiques, especially so if there aren't any monograms on the items. An Internet search for "replacement sterling patterns" will help you with this research.

When measuring sterling, always keep in mind that sterling is silver that is 0.925 fine. In order to find the melt value (if you were going this route), you would go to Kitco.com (*www.kitco.com*) to look up the spot price of silver, and then multiply by 0.925 (sterling's fineness).

Gold-Filled Pocket Watches

If you like this idea of searching for old silver and gold, there are other little known ways in which to get the metals. As with all of the ideas mentioned here, you are looking for net AGW and net ASW. This does *not* necessarily mean that you will be actually "melting down" the item. There are many items that are bought and sold at dealers for their actual gold weight or actual silver weight, but are *never even considered to be for melting purposes*!

Some of these items include the actual gold content of gold-filled pocket watches. It is a little known fact that gold-filled pocket watches contain high amounts of very high-quality gold. The trick to buying them is to know the size of the watch, the thickness of the plating of the gold, and the type of case of the watch. These three items are very easy to learn, and once they are mastered, it can be quite simple to go to an antique mall, antique show, secondhand store, or even to online sites such as eBay and know the AGW of a watch.

When buying gold-filled pocket watches, it is good to know that the best watches to buy are the ones marked in such a way as either "20 Yr Guaranteed," "20 Yr Warranted," or "20 Yr." These markings mean that when the watch was made, the gold plating was thick enough to last for 20 years of normal use without wearing off. This "20 Yr" mark is what you should shoot for, whereas "30 Yr" cases, or casings, were normally used on watches that cost too much to get reasonably, and "10 Yr" cases have gold plating that is just too thin to have any valuable gold content.

ALERT

There are many different maker's markings and hallmarks on gold-filled watch cases. There are some really good reference books that contain sketches of the hundred or so markings that indicate the difference between gold-filled and solid-gold watch cases. Know the difference and don't make the mistake of paying solid-gold prices for a gold-filled watch.

Once you have spotted the gold-filled markings of the pocket watch, the next thing to do is to determine its size and case type. Case types are easy: either the case is "open face," meaning the watch has its face covered by glass (which may be missing if it is a "parts or repair watch") but is out in the open to read. This type is in contrast to the hunter case, or hunting case, watch. The hunter case watch is the type that has a stem button that must be pushed down to open the cover over the watch face. Hunter case watches are sort of like a "clam case" watch, with both sides protected by gold-plated casing.

AGW of Gold-Filled Pocket Watches

Since you are going to look up the actual gold weight of the watch on the Kitco.com website, you next need to know the size of the watch. But be careful as sizes of watches can be tricky.

▼ **MEN'S WATCHES**

Size	Size Number	Case Style	AGW in Grams
Very Large	18	Hunter Case	1.3625
Very Large	18	Open Face	1.081525
Large	16	Hunter Case (most common)	1.27675
Large	16	Open Face	0.8725
Medium	14	Open Face	0.675

▼ **WOMEN'S WATCHES**

Size	Size Number	Case Style	AGW in Grams
Small-Medium	6	Hunter Case	0.57265
Small	0	Hunter Case	0.408675

You can use this chart to calculate the gold value of a watch that you might find at a shop. You may find one that needs a crystal, doesn't work, needs hands, etc. You can determine the size of the watch, the case of the watch, and the weight of the gold in the watch. Then look up the day's gold value on Kitco.com (which will be in ounces so the price has to be divided by 28.35 to get it in grams) and multiply this price by the content of the AGW in Grams (above) in the watch. You have then arrived at the gold content of the item.

If you think the idea of scavenging for gold watch cases is silly, you have been fooled; for proof go to eBay and look up "Gold-Filled Scrap." You will find vendors who have removed the movements (the actual ticking watch part) from the watch cases and are selling these cases. These watch cases oftentimes are recorded in the "gross gram" amount; in other words, an entire box of watch cases is placed on a scale and whatever the scale says its weight is, is listed in the eBay ad. You can look at past listings of gold watch cases that are sold in the $1,000-plus range for a whole box of empty watch cases. With this in mind, you can see that this is a money maker!

What do people do with the gold-filled watch cases, you may ask? They have them smelted down in a furnace to extract the pure gold and make 24-karat bars out of the gold plating. They then sell these 24-karat gold bars to other buyers and dealers or even to jewelry makers. It is a business, and since gold prices are high, it is very strong. There is money to be made at this sort of scavenging, though it may not be for everyone!

CHAPTER 17

A System That Works for You

A trading system that works for you is a key element to being successful and profitable. If you run your commodities trading as if it were a business, you will learn to keep track of the expenses that go into making profits. It would also be good if you knew that you can make a great deal of money by looking for and trading at only the best times. Lastly, you need to know that it is okay to give yourself time to learn the business of commodities trading.

Trading Is a Business!

While going about buying gold coins, ETFs, and mutual funds may seem like the end goal, you really should be thinking that your trading endeavors are part of a business. With this in mind, you will keep your business liquid enough to get you to the next trade. Just as the life blood of a retail or service business is cash, your trading business is reliant on the cash that is swirling around your bank account and your brokerage account. If you are not managing the cash in your account by properly timing trades—getting into and out of trades when a profit can be made—then you will not have the required cash and buying power to get you to your next trade.

In addition to getting into and out of trades at a profit, there is the expense of running a trading operation. If you are going into the city to visit a coin dealer to buy five 10-ounce bars of silver, then you have the expense of the train ticket or gasoline and parking. You also will incur the costs of Internet fees for your computer as well as the subscription expense of a news feed if you subscribe to one. Lastly, you should keep track of all of your equipment expenses, such as your iPad, iPhone, or laptop computer. These parts of the job are expensive but important to the business of trading commodities.

If it helps you to think of your commodities trading endeavors as a part-time home-based business, then you will be on the right track as far as keeping records of expenses and receipts. Remember, the IRS will get a copy of all of the gains that you have made in your brokerage account, your forex account, or your futures accounts. You will be taxed on the income you have generated from trading. Why not offset some of the income with the legitimate costs and expenses that went into the making of money in commodities trading?

Recording expenses can be done easily if a separate day/date notebook is kept; either a paper-based or electronic one will work fine. The idea is that you record in the book every time you perform some sort of service or maintenance for your commodities trading business. If you go to the Apple store in the nearby mall and buy an iPad, then keep the receipts and write down the expense of the equipment, carrying bag, and stylus. Mark this in the notebook on the calendar day that you purchased the equipment.

Also, you can write down the monthly Internet service fee if you subscribed to it, as well as the cup of coffee you had while out in the mall buying the equipment. Lastly, you should write down the mileage that you drove to get to the Apple store, or any train or bus fares that got you there; you may be able to deduct these expenses from your taxed income gains as well. Be sure to read IRS instructions about which expenses can be deducted from your income for tax purposes.

ESSENTIAL

You can purchase income and expense tracking software that is easy to use. You also can find scaled-down versions that can be synced to your Smartphone and tablet computer. This way you will be able to take notes and keep track of expenses even when you are out and about.

The idea is that you will have complete and accurate records of what it actually costs you to generate income. If this means a trip to the antique mall to look for scrap gold-filled pocket watches, then this means keeping track of your mileage to the antique store, the monthly Internet fees of your iPad or handheld unit to check the market price of gold, the costs of the book you just bought that illustrate all of the gold and gold-filled hallmarks, and lunch out at your favorite country café.

Many of these expenses are legitimate costs of doing business, not to mention the actual cost of the gold or silver that you buy if you purchase any. The idea is that you are in business. This means that the income you make can be offset with the legitimate expenses that it takes you to make the income. Good records are the key. Again, make sure you follow IRS guidelines carefully so that you have accurate records and know which specific expenses can be deducted from income.

Get Ready to Trade by Studying

Before you place your first trade for the day, you should have a routine of how you get to the point of seeing whether there is an actual opportunity in the commodities market. You should have in your mind the saying, "Study the market first, trade second." Just like the expert in any other field, including buyers for retail establishments that take in goods over the counter, it is best for you to know commodities or at least one or two commodities well enough to be able to recognize a "deal" when you see one. Being able to spot buying and shorting opportunities is crucial to making money in the market.

If you are a short-time trader, you have to sit on the sidelines for a day or two waiting for a news story to develop that reflects when there is a good entry point in the price of a leveraged ETF. On the other hand, if you are a long-term trader and have been building up your gold and silver position over the past nine months, you may decide to wait until the Chinese New Year season is over before you reenter the gold-coin or silver-bullion market.

You will have to know when is a good time to trade your cash for oil, copper, corn, or cocoa. You will need to know when the time is right, that it is a good setup, and that you have a reasonable expectation that the trade will go well.

ALERT

It is very easy to lose your place in the fast-moving world of commodities and trading in the markets. If you keep a reading plan that is scheduled, you will stay on top of the big picture as well as the small picture. Take every opportunity to read and find time to fit market study into your busy day.

Acquiring this level of knowledge takes a bit of study of the fundamentals and the charts. As you build up your expertise, you can get into a routine of tracking the goings on in the world very easily. At first it will take a lot of work for you to try to absorb as much information and learning as possible. As you grow in knowledge, you can settle into a routine that suits your lifestyle.

The idea is that you get a head of steam going with your knowledge, and then you let it slowly simmer for months and months. It can be very rewarding to read about a developing story and then have the trading opportunity appear right before your eyes on your computer weeks later. At the same time, it can be a good feeling to walk through a secondhand store and know that the price of gold is set to go up in the next six months, and that while the price of the old gold pendant you are looking at is high, it will seem cheap in a few months. Learning leads to knowledge, and this knowledge can compound in depth if built up over time.

Look for the Perfect Setup

One of the key differences between professional traders and amateurs is the fact that professionals will be able to wait out a market that doesn't look good. Since these professional traders rely on their trading expertise and on their own (or their company's) money to make a living at it, they naturally are very reluctant to get into a trade that doesn't have a reasonable expectation of turning a profit.

An amateur trader, on the other hand, may mistakenly have this sense that he must be trading all of the time. There are tales of young traders who buy and sell so often that there is almost no hope of even 50 percent of their trades working in their favor. These amateur traders lose their sense of here and there, and their brokerage accounts get smaller and smaller with each trading day. Instead of waiting for the best time and best opportunity, they trade at every opportunity, good or bad.

Perhaps this overtrading is brought on by inadequate experience, or perhaps it is brought on by the enchantment of the act of trading. Either way, a professional is a professional, and needs to be assured that her trades will work out. This working out of trades leads directly to her paycheck that will pay her rent or mortgage. Add to this the fact that if a trader does not win at trading then she is losing, in which case her account balance will go down and down over time. The result is a very cautious trader indeed!

Some trading houses are set up so that the trader uses the company's money. Other trading houses are set up like partnerships, where each trader buys in to the ownership of the firm and therefore shares with the profits of all of the other owners/traders. This latter type is called a *proprietary trading firm*, and is most like your own trading business model.

So the adage, "Look before you leap!" also applies very well to trading and should be a bit of wisdom you adhere to when you get the itch to trade. Searching for setups is actually the most difficult part of trading. You must look through all of the information, charts, and news, and then filter it to see if there really is a setup available. Setups are the key to profitable trading. If there are no setups, then there can be no profits. This means that if there are no setups available, there should be no trading for that day.

You can train yourself to walk away from your trading if there aren't any opportunities. If you are still eager to trade, then by all means shut off your computer and take a walk to the nearest coffee house. Get out of your environment in order to shake off the idea that you must trade today; otherwise you will find yourself forcing the trade. These times are perfect for going to the gym, taking a hike, or even going to the mall. The money you spend at golf or on a shopping trip will go to far better use than if you were to lose money trying to force a profit on a bad trading day.

This is the business of trading: Some days there is money to be made in the market; some days it is better just to go to the beach! Even if you broke up your electronic trading with a trip to the local junk shop to look for pocket watches or old jewelry, you would be better off than forcing bad trades. The idea is to break out of the thought that you must trade. What you must do is look for setups and *then* trade: No setups, no trades. If the market is not going anywhere, or is **flat** as it is called, then your money will be wasted in a trade. In fact, your money also will be at risk, as when the market is flat and there is change in the wind, with the direction of the commodity soon to go up or down. If, however, you can read into the charts and news and determine which direction that the raw materials price will go next, then by all means buy into the trade.

If you don't know or aren't 100 percent in the know, then you have earned yourself a day off. You may ask yourself, how can I make money by not trading? How can I have a profit unless I make this trade? Your answer is that the profit you make is the money that you saved by not taking chances in a market that didn't have a clear direction.

Funding Your Account

Your trading account and the money you use to buy the gold and silver at coin dealers is real money. It may seem strange to mention this, but many people still seem to lose track of this fact when they plunk down a stack of $20 bills to buy a gold Swiss 20 Franc (0.1867 ounces of gold), or when they mail in a check to their brokerage firm. Money is strange, as money can be defined by what it can buy. If the money that you trade with is used to buy leveraged aluminum ETFs, then this is not the same money that can be used to make the payment on your new Mercedes Benz. If you like to frequent fancy restaurants and order drinks with your dinner, then this money can't be used to buy a commodities mutual fund or load up on U.S. pre-1964 90 percent silver quarters.

The money in your position can go both ways: it can be used, or it can be saved and used to invest or trade with. If you are trying to get into trading, then you will quickly realize that you will be able to make more money with each trade if the size of the trade is bigger. In other words, you will need to have a certain-size dollar balance in your account to get to the point that when your trades gain 2 percent, 3 percent, or 4 percent, the size of those gains are big enough to make a difference.

In order to do this, you will need money. Here comes the choice: You can choose to build up your trading account with the money that is diverted away from other purposes. Everyone has heard about how much you can save by cutting down on visits to your local coffee shop. At the same time, how many people have heard of the trader who is holding off buying himself a BMW convertible because "it will take too much money out of my trading account"?

ESSENTIAL

Money used to build up your trading account can go both ways: It may be a high priority if you are thinking of using commodities trading to draw paychecks from. Or it may be a casual buildup, such as when you include commodities in your overall investment portfolio and you are dollar cost averaging into a commodities mutual fund.

Getting to the point in which you become a professional trader takes dedication and talent. It also takes dedication and talent to get to the point where you actually have a good-sized balance in your trading account! Putting money aside is hard, and understandably so. If you are saving for retirement and are building up a position in commodities as a part of your overall retirement plan, then perhaps it is easier to put that money away. No matter, the fact remains that more money in your account or more money in your wallet would allow you to buy bigger bites of the commodities apple when the time came. Wouldn't you like to have enough to buy 10 ounces of silver when the price drops $3.50 in one afternoon instead of buying just 3 or 5 ounces of silver? Remember, the price of silver is more than $30 an ounce, and at this writing it continuously closes in on $40 per ounce. This means you would need $400 in cash to buy 10 ounces of silver, as opposed to needing $120 to buy just 3 ounces of silver. Wait, you might say, I don't even have the $120! If this is the case, then perhaps you can look around and make some adjustments. Perhaps it means making only one trip to the coffee shop when you are at work, and not three trips as you normally would. Perhaps it means not buying so many pairs of shoes. You know who you are! If the goal is to buy commodities, then you will need money to do so. If you feel like you would have extra money to buy and sell with, why not move that higher up on your priority list?

Giving Yourself a Paycheck

If you are trading short term, you should be looking at your monthly performance in percentages. If you are trading longer term, you could check your performance every six to nine months. The idea is to match the holding period of the assets with the time period you are observing. It would not do justice to yourself to look at how much you have made in the market every few days if you are thinking of holding your investment for a quarter, a year, or for several years. At the same time, you will need to monitor your investing progress if you are in and out of your trades every day or so, or even every week.

The smallest time frame for monitoring your trading when considering whether to draw paychecks should be a month. This will give the law of averages time to work and smooth out any extreme high returning trades with any losing trades. Also, the monthly check-in for profits coincides with a normal pay period as if you were working a normal job. With this in mind, you can look at your profits for the month and then decide if you want to take some of your profits from your account to give yourself a paycheck.

Remember, you are running the trading operation like a business. This means a paycheck for a job well done. It also means taking money out of your profits, but it is going to be used to pay for living expenses.

ESSENTIAL

You don't have to draw a paycheck out of your account if you don't want to. If you would like to see your money grow, then the best thing you can do is to take out money for your expenses, but let the profits compound. The rolled-over profits will add up very quickly over time!

If you have gross trading income of $250 for a month, but it cost you $50 for Internet service, $75 for equipment such as your iPad, and $32 in periodicals such as the *Wall Street Journal* and a few magazines, you can take money out of the account to "repay" yourself for the expenses. If you have kept track of what it cost you to make that money, then you will know how much you need to withdraw to pay your expenses. In any business, income minus expenses equals profits. Make sure you pay yourself back for the withdrawals that have come out of your own pocket to keep up the business of trading. Make such a withdrawal every month. Don't fall into the habit of continually feeding the business with your personal funds; your trading business should be self-sustaining. This may be a high goal to reach, but this is the ideal situation for a trading operation.

How Much Profit Is Okay?

Once you begin to trade commodities you will start to wonder how much profit is normal. You will wonder if the seemingly small amount you made your first month is even worth the effort it takes to get up and running and learn all of the things about trading that you need to know.

You can start with the idea that it is okay to have a period of trading in which you only break even. You may discover that trading is difficult at first, that you have gotten yourself into a few trades that didn't work out as planned, and that you were lucky to get out with any account left at all. Other trades may not have been so good, or if there was a profit, you weren't sure how it worked out at all!

So getting up and running takes a bit of expertise and experience. It also takes some time in the saddle and with this come the inevitable wins and losses. Giving yourself a break-in period, allowing yourself time to learn the ropes, and ease into trading will go a long way in keeping yourself in the trading game. This doesn't mean giving yourself money to burn and to waste on trades that never would have worked out. What it does mean is that you give yourself a break when things go bad.

Getting down on yourself is not good, but it seems hard to get away from those types of feelings when an ETF just sits there day after day, or the futures goes in the wrong direction, or the scrap gold you bought turns out not to be worth as much as you had planned.

When this happens, cheer up! You are in the big leagues, trading for a profit. Most people just trade for fun, with no plan or idea of entry and exit points. Most people will not have a plan about what to do with a copper

ETF or an oil futures, or even know to buy gold on Mondays because the price always seems to go down on Mondays.

Even the fact that you are aware of your losses and wonder why a trade didn't work out puts you way ahead of most investors and traders. Most will be looking at the world with a "tell me" attitude and will accept all that they hear without even knowing enough or caring enough to think for themselves and discriminate. Most people will not attempt to look for setups or know how to wait for the right time to trade and to sit on their hands when the time is bad. It takes time to learn how to hold on to a trade that pulls back, and then wait for it to creep back into the green profit zone, slowly but surely. Give yourself a break, go slowly, keep reading, and keep looking for setups. Trading is a skill that can be learned. Keep learning and you will do well!

CHAPTER 18

The Cash Account, Futures, Futures Options

This chapter will discuss how to think about keeping your trading account as a cash account for safety and liquidity. It will also discuss how you should get acquainted with the price of commodities before trading if you haven't looked in the market in a while. Lastly, the concept of how commodities futures and commodities futures options are traded and used is covered.

Keeping It Liquid, Keeping It in Cash

Trading commodities means starting with your account in cash, looking for setups, moving into the trade, and then moving out of the trade and back into cash. The most important element in this equation is the being in cash part. If you are trading short term, being *in cash* should be your primary goal. Just sitting in cash during a bad market can have the effect of earning money. In these cases, the money will be earned by not risking it in a trade that has a good chance of going bad. Sometimes the money you make is the money you haven't risked unnecessarily.

Taking this idea further, professional traders often get to the point in their careers that they don't think, "How much will I make today?" They will rather think, "How much am I not going to lose today?" This is a curious difference as the idea of winning in the market is overshadowed with the fear of losing in the market. Take this as an example of the mindset that a professional trader has when approaching the trading day.

The Risks of Trading

Accepting risk is the business of trading. Even if you are buying gold bars and waiting for a worst-case scenario in the world's banking sector, there will still be the risk that the gold will be of less value in dollars at the end of its investment period as it was planned to be when bought. This is the inherent risk of trading. Of course, the risks of trading can be lessened with the time of the trade.

ESSENTIAL

The risk of a trade can be broken down into three categories: low, medium, and high. One method of keeping risk low is to divide your account into three "buckets." The low-risk bucket will be general commodities mutual funds and ETFs. The medium-risk bucket is the leveraged ETFs. The high-risk bucket would be the futures and futures options.

The risks of trading can be lessened by a very short trade, such as one that is in and out within a week. The risks can also be lessened with the long end of the time spectrum. This means that if you are investing for a time frame such as five, seven, or more years, there is a greater chance that the price of the commodity will gain over the long haul and the trade will turn out to be a gain at the end.

Cash Is King

With cash, you will be following the same process in both the short term and the long term: cash, commodity, back to cash. If it helps to think of your trading account as a cash account, then go ahead and think of it that way. After all is said and done, it is cash that pays your bills, cash that pays the mortgage, and cash that buys the groceries. While entering into a commodities trade can earn you money, it is good to keep the focus that you can't pay your bills with a barrel of oil, a bar of gold, or a bushel of corn. These are the traded goods, and the purpose of trading them is for you to get to the point where you will have more money in your account at the end of the trade.

Carrying this further, if it is cash you want, then by all means, stay in cash as long as possible. This is why it is good to think of your account as a cash account, and the trading you are doing as reinforcement to your otherwise strong cash position. If you are thinking short term, this position can easily be thought through, as the account will be going in and out of cash many times during a trading month.

This concept of your account having a primary function of being a cash account is easier if you are trading for income. If you are trading for income, you will quickly associate the gains in your account with the cash paycheck that you are drawing out with each pay period.

Keeping Tabs on the Prices

If you have built up a strong knowledge in commodities, you will be able to go day to day with just a refresher each morning as to the current data and charts of the trading day. It might mean that you follow the markets by reading *The Economist*, logging into the CNBC app on your tablet computer, or watching Bloomberg in the early morning hours.

Your learning will go much easier if you pick a few sectors of the commodities world that you can relate to better than others. If you really want to trade corn, because you grew up in rural America, then focus on this food commodity. If you like the idea of going to coin shops to sort through piles of 1-ounce silver art bars to add to your collection, then follow the gold and silver markets. If you like the idea of hedging the fuel costs of your family's summer trip by going along with a leveraged gasoline ETF, then follow the news that is generated about the Brent North Sea crude oil or the prices of West Texas Intermediate (WTI) crude.

Monitoring the price of the commodity on a daily basis will keep you on top of the elements that go into the pricing of these raw materials. If you follow the news, you will know that there is a bubble in the price of oil, and that this is built up due to traders running up the markets and that it might be time to short oil.

At the same time, if you have been away from trading for a while, then the prices of the commodities you were so keen on watching might shock you. Prices have a tendency to be moving all of the time. If you trade oil and you were last looking at oil being $80 dollars a barrel with talk and technicals of it going to $90, then this is what you will be expecting when you tune back into the markets after a break from trading. Say, for example, that you have had a successful run trading oil ETFs but have gotten out of the market due to a heavy school, work, or home schedule. Say it has been two months since you have looked at your computer and your trading websites, as a family or work matter has taken a front seat to your attention.

ALERT

Keeping out of the market during busy times in your life may be one of the best things you can do for yourself and your account. Trading commodities can be stressful. If you are too busy or are not able to enjoy trading, then it is perfectly fine to walk away for a few months at a time.

After a time away from trading, you will have to ease into the new prices that you will see on your quote screen. It may be that the oil that was sure to go to $90 actually went to $115! You would then naturally think, wait, $115? That's too high; it should be at $90, so I'll short it and make a ton!

The fact is that there probably is a really good reason that oil reached $115 a barrel, and you will have to build a new "model" as to what will be a fair price in the future. It may still be a fact that oil (or any other commodity) has run up in price too fast and is in a state that is nearing correction.

So with this said, after time off from the trading world, look at the new price of the commodity with a fresh perspective. It may be that the price has changed for a good reason, and it is fairly priced according to the latest market conditions. Prices of commodities come and go with the change of a headline. It sometimes seems that the changes are so gradual that you will not notice them unless you have walked away from them for a while. If you haven't looked at the price of a commodity for some time, look again. It might be a very different price than you remembered it to be, which, if not fully absorbed into your pricing model, could result in a trade that is placed on the wrong side, resulting in a loss in your account.

To sum up, always allow time to get readjusted to commodities prices when returning to trading after a time away from daily study of the news that relates to commodity prices.

The Value of Commodities Trading

If you are building your commodities trading business into one that serves your needs, then trading commodities is doing its job. Your needs might be to have a place to go on a Saturday afternoon. You may decide that you like the social interaction of going to the antique flea markets in your area on an otherwise boring Saturday afternoon. You may find that you like to cruise through the tables full of stuff, digging down deep for sterling and gold to buy on the cheap.

You might also find that there is a social aspect of being able to discuss the market and your trading with your friends at the gym. Maybe you like the ability to make your own decisions about how to invest your money without having to rely on your know-it-all brother-in-law! Any way you look at it, if you are getting out of commodities trading what you need, then the process of learning the market, entering and exiting trades, building up knowledge, and learning how to manage risk is valuable to your life.

How much money do you need to get started in commodities trading? While it usually takes a minimum of $1,000 to buy into a commodities mutual fund, and $20,000 on average to get a commodities trading advisor, you can get your first position in silver for about $4. This would buy you one U.S. pre-1964, 90 percent silver dime!

Even if you are a very, very small-time player and only have 1-ounce of silver in your entire commodities portfolio, you will still be in on the game. The buy-in with commodities is very small; even with the purchase and sorting of pennies you can be a player in the copper market. This "in the market" can lead to a real interest that can further lead to a real knowledge of investing, trading, economics, and central bank data.

It is said that if you really want to learn, you should be able to do so as cheaply as possible. You can go to the public library to access the Internet sites that are listed in this book. You do not need to have a Smartphone, laptop, or iPad to be in the commodities market. You don't even need a brokerage account. You can go into a coin dealer and buy a roll of U.S. pre-1964, 90 percent silver dimes or quarters for the price of a movie and popcorn for two.

On the other hand, you can build your commodities trading skills to the point where you are trading full time. There is a certain romance about being able to make money with money, and if it is part of the trading market, and something people can relate to such as foodstuffs, heating oil, gasoline, or even gold, then so much the better. There is also a romance to running a tight little trading business that earns its keep, pays for its own expenses, and even gives you a good lifestyle to boot. Maybe it is the feeling that you are able to control what seems to be impossible to control:

your money and your emotions relating to money. Either way, only you can decide what value commodities trading adds to your life. If the benefits go beyond the financial gains you make, then commodities trading is that much better.

A Bit about Futures

This book has given some insight into futures trading. Futures trading is a specialized art form and can be covered in its own book to explore all of the tips and techniques. While most of the trading ideas in this book were presented with a normal brokerage trading account in mind, there was also some mention of futures. The basics of futures are described next.

People who trade in the futures market are actually trading electronic versions of legal contracts. The contract will contain an element that is based on the price of the underlying. This **underlying** is a specific size, product, quality of product, and expiration date of commodity product. The contract states that the owner of the contract has the right to buy or sell the specific product named in the contract at a specific date in the future.

There are a specific number of units per contract, such as a specific number of ounces of gold, bushels of corn, or barrels of oil. The date in the future is the date that the contract will come due. While each contract will expire at the due date (and therefore it settles for final value,) it is possible to trade the contracts anytime right up until their expiration dates.

With each contract set for specific times, amounts, and products, there is a hedger and a speculator. If you are a commodities futures trader, you will be the **speculator**. The speculator is the contract holder who speculates that the price of his particular commodity will be higher or lower at the time his contract comes due, thus resulting in a profit for him. The speculator doesn't think of ever actually owning the corn, wheat, or oil in the futures contract (as opposed to the hedger who produces or needs to take delivery of the commodity in the future for business purposes.) The **hedger** will be the farmer who is attempting to lock in the profits of his corn crop, even though the price of a bushel of corn at the end of the growing season is not known. Other examples of hedgers would be an airline that is managing the price of jet fuel costs six months in the future, or a food company managing the cost of the grains it uses to produce the finished food good it will sell to grocery stores.

FACT

Many companies use commodities hedging with futures as a form of insurance against rising fuel and food costs. Companies such as airlines hedge with futures successfully. Better forecasting of fuel cost means better management, one of the most difficult elements in the expense side of the airline's profitability.

In this case the farmer will know the minimum price he will need to charge for his corn in order for it to be profitable for him to farm corn. He will enter into a corn futures contract that will be set up in such a way that he will make money when the price of corn falls below his pre-determined level. In this way, he will be losing money when he brings his actual corn to market in the fall. When he drives his truck to the grain bins during harvest, he will get market price. If the market price is below what he needs as his bottom price, he will be at a loss. At the same time, his futures contract will be 100 percent offsetting to the movement of the actual corn price in the opposite direction. This means that the futures contract that he entered into in the spring will be in a profit exactly enough to offset his losses. The net result is a loss and a gain of equal value, and hence, a locked-in price for the corn.

The farmer's profit is assured by using these futures contracts. In other words, the hedger (farmer) will set up the futures trade to make money at the exact same rate and volume that he will be losing money if he bought (or sold) the commodity in the market. The hedge will be at a 1:1 ratio, with $1 gained in the futures market for every $1 lost in the actual cash market. The net result at the end of the trade is a gain of $0. In this case the farmer might lose $25,000 when selling the actual corn in the market, but his futures contract will be set up to work in the opposite direction, and will gain $25,000 (hence the 1:1 relationship) resulting in a "locked in profit point." This is actually a sophisticated management tool that can mean the difference between profits or not at some of the largest airlines, food companies, and manufactures worldwide.

Your Side of the Futures Contract

When you enter into a futures contract, you will be either long or short. You will earn or lose on a daily basis as the time of the contract winds down to its expiration date. Each day you will be either up or down. If you are up, the profits will be added to your account in cash. If you are down, the losses will be subtracted from your account in cash. The net effect is that no trader ever is allowed to run his account down to the point of no return. If the account falls below the minimum margin, the trading house will automatically close out the account, and you will be stuck with the loss. If this happens, it is called a ***margin call***.

You may get a fair warning about the margin call, and you may have until the end of the trading day to bring the balance of the account to the minimum level to prevent the closing of positions. The automatic closing of positions is a bad thing and should be avoided because once you are closed out, there is no chance that you will be able to gain if the commodity moves up in price the next day. If you are out, you're out and it's game over!

The best way to avoid this is to limit the size of your trades to fit your overall account size. Too big a position will wipe out any account in a hurry! At the end of the contract, both sides will settle up. You do not need to take possession of the corn, oil, cocoa, or heating oil; rather, you close out the trade with an opposite trade, lock in your profits, and get the difference in cash settled into your account. Closing with an opposite trade is easier to do than it sounds and is actually what is going on behind the scenes in the trading software when you click on the button "close trade." It is actually a netting the shorts with the longs and results in a zero exposure of the commodity contract.

Futures are traded on both an open outcry system and in an electronic format. The ***open outcry system*** is the old system of masses of traders in tiered circles where specific commodities and other financial products are traded. These traders use a system of hand signals, shouting, and handheld gizmos to trade millions of dollars of commodities per day. These are the men and women in the colorful jackets who are shown in the background when CNBC shows the trading floors. The exchanges in Chicago have viewing windows for those who want to see the action in person.

ESSENTIAL

Keep a lookout for the floor traders when you are watching news reports on CNBC. The easiest time to see floor traders is when CNBC is giving a live report on bond prices. This report comes on once an hour and is filmed with live trading pits in the background.

The ***electronic trading method*** is one of logging into a computer, entering your trade with a trading platform, and earning your profits.

Trading futures has some obstacles. One of the biggest is the complexity of the margin system. Trading futures means trading on leverage. This gives added boost to your buying power, which means you can buy 10× to 20× (ten times to twenty times) as much of the futures contract as you could buy if you had a normal ETF trading account with the same cash balance. In other words, futures trading can be leveraged 10:1 or 20:1 depending on the contract.

This boost to your buying power can lead to spectacular returns in your futures account when there are profits. By the same token, the losses in a futures account can be equally as spectacular; the leverage sword cuts both ways, for both wins and losses.

With this in mind, approach futures trading with care, as there is a lot of money to be made or lost in this market. Again, start with a demo or practice trading account to get a feel for how the daily settlement system works, or how the margin will affect your account for good and bad. Get some practice before trying out this dynamic and exciting way of trading commodities.

Contract Specs and Futures Options

Commodities futures are traded on exchanges in New York, Chicago, and London. It can be very difficult to access the London exchange, so most of the futures traders in the United States use their online futures brokerage accounts to access the New York or Chicago exchanges. Different commodities are traded on different exchanges. A list of some common commodities contracts and their specifics are listed below.

Commodity	Contract Size	Exchange	Trading Hours
Light Sweet Crude	1,000 barrels	NYMEX	10 A.M. – 2:30 Eastern
Heating Oil #2	42,000 gallons	NYMEX	10 A.M. – 2:30 Eastern
Gasoline: NY Unleaded	42,000 gallons	NYMEX	10:05 A.M. – 2:30 Eastern
Natural Gas	10,000 million BTUs	NYMEX	10 A.M. – 2:30 Eastern
Copper	25,000 pounds	CMX	8:10 A.M. – 1 P.M. Eastern
Silver	5,000 troy ounces	CMX	8:25 A.M. – 1:25 Eastern
Soybeans	5,000 bushels	CBOT	9:30 A.M. – 1:15 P.M. Central
Oats	5,000 bushels	CBOT	9:30 A.M. – 1:15 Central
Corn	5,000 bushels	CBOT	9:30 A.M. – 1:15 Central

There is another option to trading commodities that offers a large income potential versus the size of the account. This refers to the trading of futures options. ***Futures options*** are just that—options on futures. In other words, they are traded and priced exactly like options on stocks (the common form) but are options on futures. Their price will move up and down on the up and down of the price of the future contract that they are tied to, not to a stock like a stock option. In all other aspects, such as the complex time element of their pricing and trading strategies, futures options are the same as stock options. Since they are based on future prices, the value of the option will be tied to the value in the future, as the option uses the future as an underlying. This underlying future has its price tied to the price of the actual commodity. Futures options are perhaps the most complex way to trade commodities.

These commodities futures options are best traded with complex strategies that involve calls, puts, and premiums. With an option you are paying for the right, but not the obligation, to buy or sell the futures contract in the future. The amount of time left on the option before it expires is an element in the options value. Obviously, the longer the time there is on the option, the more time there will be for the option to become of greater and greater profit. Therefore, the time left on the option is called a **time premium**.

Lastly, if you like trading options you have the opportunity to engage in some really complex strategies. These strategies make money in up markets, down markets, and markets that are stuck in the mud. These strategies are called **condors and straddles**.

If you think you would like to get into trading futures options, do some reading or take an online training class. These are offered for free at the CBOE (Chicago Board Options Exchange) website (*www.cboe.com*). Look carefully into futures options trading before you begin, as this can be one of the most aggressive ways to trade commodities.

CHAPTER 19

Investing Indirectly

Sometimes the only way you are able to invest in commodities is indirectly. You may not be able to or care to trade futures. You may not want to buy and store gold and silver in your home safe. You may want an easier way to manage and a simpler form of investing that will still yield exposure to the future growth and gains in raw materials. This chapter will give you some alternate choices for your commodities portfolio.

Commodities Mutual Funds

There are other methods of investing in the commodities markets besides the direct methods such as futures and actual physical gold, silver, and copper. One of the easiest ways to build a position in the commodities markets is by investing in a commodity mutual fund. **Commodity mutual funds** are set up just like other mutual funds in the market, including bond, equity, and sector funds such as technology funds.

Factors to consider when investing in a mutual fund include whether the fund has a load or not and what the minimum purchase amount is.

ESSENTIAL

A search on Google Finance for "Commodity" and then "Funds" leads to a list of mutual funds that are invested in commodities and raw materials. You can call up this list of funds and sort through them to look for those that best suit your needs.

When a mutual fund has a **load**, this means that the mutual fund has a sales charge associated with it; this sales charge theoretically is the price you will pay your financial advisor for giving you financial advice. While most every personal finance book and website recommends against loaded funds as charging unnecessary fees (called sales fees or loads), it is more acceptable to consider them if you are using the services of a financial advisor. These financial advisors derive their income from giving clients appropriate advice: Thus, you may consider it appropriate to compensate them through the purchase of a "loaded fund" or one that has a sales charge associated with it.

Although even the smallest mutual-fund houses will offer basic stock and bond funds, you should keep in mind that most of the commodities mutual funds on the market will be offered through major mutual-fund houses. With that being said, there will be similarities in the performance of each fund in relation to the commodities market in general. To put it mildly, if there is a high percentage of the mutual fund invested in gold, gold miners, oil, and oil companies, and these commodities are set to have a good year (or five- to seven-year time frame if you are looking at a complete investment cycle), then there is a really good chance that these funds will do well also.

It is best to look into a mutual fund that has a composition of commodities that are somewhat linked to an index or following a commodity index. With this method of screening mutual funds, you will ensure that the mutual fund that you are about to invest in is not too heavily invested into one area of the commodities market. While a fund manager might think that the copper market is set to take off, a fund that has an "overweight" in copper stocks and copper futures precludes the basic notion that a mutual fund is designed to offer diversification of an investment, even if that investment is within a very tight investment sector.

ETFs

ETFs and Commodity ETF basics have been covered in an earlier chapter. While the subjects of diversified ETFs that follow a commodities index were mentioned before, there are more aggressive ways to use the concept of the commodity ETF in an investment or trading portfolio.

One of the best methods of adding more return to a commodity investment is to buy and trade commodity ETFs that are focused on only one area of the commodity index. With this in mind, you can analyze the gold market, and go long with a leveraged 3x gold ETF such as the Direxion Daily Gold Miners Bull 2x (symbol NUGT) when you are thinking the gold market is about to break out. On the other hand, you can buy shares of the ETF Direxion Daily Gold Miners Bear 3x (symbol DUST) if you think that the price of gold will go down in the next few days.

These leveraged ETFs use margin within the ETF to buy double the amount of the gold miner stocks in the fund. In this case, they act as if you were buying twice the amount for the 2x fund and triple the amount for the 3x fund as the amount of securities in a normal ETF for the same amount of money. This also means that if the market moves against you, these funds will work against you just as fast! Watch out when using 2x or 3x ETFs in your trading. Make sure that the direction the ETF will move is very clear, and you are sure of your trade before you buy.

ALERT

The compounding effect of leveraged ETFs is not as potent after a few days (due to the negating effect of the up and down of the underlying commodity or stocks in the ETF). With this in mind, 2x and 3xs are best used to get into and out of a trading situation in hours or days and no longer.

These leveraged gold miners ETFs are a trader's dream, as the gold miner stocks can be very volatile when the physical gold market is moving. One real world example occurred on the close of Friday, January 27, 2012. The gold ETF GLD moved up 1.02 percent while the 3x gold miner's ETF "NUGT" moved up 6.92 percent, almost 700 percent more than the movement of the gold bullion itself! As you can see, these leveraged ETFs can be a real money maker—*if* they are handled correctly.

Focused ETFs

If you are interested in the concept of the very focused, leveraged ETF you can choose one that invests in oil and gas, basic materials (lumber, nickel, and iron ore), agriculture commodities and stocks, base metals, copper, silver, etc. A comprehensive list can be found by doing an internet search for "Leveraged ETFs."

Of course, you can build a much tamer investment portfolio of ETFs that are not leveraged, but are still separated into the different sections of the commodities index. These are just like all other commodities ETFs but they are focused within only one area of the commodities index. These work for all aspects of the commodities spectrum, whether it is gold, oil, grains, or the base metals such as copper, iron, and nickel. You can buy a series of ETFs in the sectors of the commodities index that you think are going to move ahead in the investment world. If the world's economies are beginning to come out of a recession, or are beginning to ramp up, copper and oil would be good bets. You could add them to your portfolio by owning ETFs that are invested in copper futures and copper mining stocks. The same is true for all other types of commodities: You can build an individual portfolio of ETFs that are invested in separate parts of the commodities index.

FACT

Full-service firms often issue mid- to long-term outlooks on the individual components of the commodities index. The mid- to long-term outlooks usually recommend an area of the commodities index as well as buy and sell points (along with the reasoning behind the investment).

If you were thinking of using these focused ETFs, then it would be best to do your research before building up too big a position in a subgroup of raw materials. This is especially true during the different seasons of the year: During the spring months, you could begin to accumulate oil and energy ETFs, and during the fall and winter months you could accumulate gold, gold miner ETFs, and silver ETFs.

Another option is that you could accumulate and trade grain-based ETFs at the beginning of the growing season. If you are thinking of going with grains, it is best to go heavy with the recommendations of your full-service broker. UBS, Goldman Sachs, and some of the other commodities brokerage firms will offer direction and advice as to entry points and exit points of what grain funds to buy and when.

ESSENTIAL

Brokerage firms such as UBS might issue guidance as to the potential price of cocoa, corn, or sugar. The firm will give price predictions for three, six, and twelve months out based on their models of where those product prices will be at those points in the future. They derive this information based on the product growing conditions, worldwide macro-economic conditions, and current futures pricing.

Since predicting the future price of any asset can be difficult, having a source such as these brokers' reports to guide you can really help you in setting up a direction in which to take your trading and investing. While the process is flawed and not 100 percent accurate all of the time, these brokers' reports from futures dealers and full-service firms will give you a baseline in which to begin your trading and accumulation of these assets.

Individual Commodity Company Stocks

One of the easiest (and some say the safest) methods of investing in commodities is buying stock in the companies that are commodities' producers. Since most of these companies are well established and have older developed product lines, they will fall into the category of "value" stocks. If you are of traditional investment mind, you will do well by buying stock in companies such as Archer Daniels Midland Company (ADM), BP, and Rio Tinto (RIO). These companies grow grains, drill for oil, and mine minerals. Many of them have been around for most of last century and have stood the test of time, through tech bubbles, bank failures, and housing crashes.

FACT

A firm's staying power and product line are important to investment potential. Research in Motion (RIM), which makes the BlackBerry, was a market darling a few years ago. These days, however, RIM's stock has taken a very far back seat to Apple Inc. (AAPL), after the introduction of its iPhone. Rio Tinto, on the other hand, is strong and has been mining gold, silver, diamonds, and iron ore all over the world for more than 100 years!

Since these companies are well established, when they are profitable, they will return some of the money the company has made back to their investors in the form of dividends. Sometimes the dividends can be the same amount of a bond, but the stock also has the ability to move up with the ramping up of the commodities and the stock markets in general.

These commodity company stocks can really be very high-quality investments compared to some of the more popular stocks of the day. Sometimes the basics make the best investments, and a stock that makes, grows, mines, or drills for the basic raw materials can be one of the key components in your commodities portfolio.

Add a company's dividends to its staying power and strong product line, and you have a very high-quality, lower-risk investment vehicle that anyone would be proud to have in their brokerage account.

If you would like to add commodity stocks to your investment portfolio, then you can be a bit more lenient as to the percentage of your overall investable assets that are in commodities. This is true because these commodity stocks are really classified as stocks and equities, even though they fall into the category of commodity assets. They act as kind of a blend of the two risk categories: the low risk of a value stock (*value stocks* being ones that pay high dividends) and at the same time part of the raw materials business.

You can find a list of companies that offer commodity stocks by doing a bit of research. One of the best places to look is to find a commodity ETF's website and look at the investment companies that are contained in that ETF. Make a note of them and do an Internet search through Google Finance to get the particulars on these companies. You can then carry the process further by searching through brokers' reports on the individual companies for the brokers' recommendations.

Commodity Currencies as a Proxy

One of the most exotic and rewarding ways to invest in commodities is to buy, hold, and trade the currencies of the world's commodity-producing nations. This works out to be a good investment because the price of the money used by countries that mine, grow, or drill for natural recourses will gain against the currency used by the country that buys these commodities.

It works like this: countries like Japan will buy raw materials from other commodity-producing nations such as New Zealand. If a Japanese food producer wants to buy grains from a New Zealand grower, the food producer must first use his Japanese yen to buy New Zealand dollars on the open market. That food producer will then use New Zealand dollars to pay the grain supplier for the grain. Although one currency transaction has a tiny effect, a whole nation of Japanese buyers converting yen into New Zealand dollars will have the effect of pushing down the value of mass amounts of Japanese yen sold and pushing up the value of the mass amounts of New Zealand dollars bought (due to the amount of buying and selling in the open market).

Carrying the process further, if you consider that grains, metals, and fuel will go up in price, then you will buy currencies of the countries that produce these raw materials; by doing so you will earn money against the price of the currency of countries that use and consume these commodities. You would need a means to buy Australian dollars, Canadian dollars, New Zealand dollars, and Norwegian kroner.

ESSENTIAL

Trading in commodity currencies (or currencies from countries that produce and export large amounts of commodities in relation to the amounts of their other exports) in a traditional forex account can be very complex and very risky, but also very rewarding and profitable! If you are interested in the subject, read the book titled *The Everything® Guide to Currency Trading*, also written by this author.

The more complex route would be to trade forex in a traditional currency account. At the same time, the process can be somewhat simplified by the purchase of an ETF. Much like a commodities ETF, these currency ETFs are invested in cash and money markets of other countries' currencies.

While not perfect, these currency ETFs offer an easy way to buy into two of the heaviest hitters in the commodity currency world, the Australian dollar and the Canadian dollar. These ETFs symbols are FXA for the Australian dollar and FXC for the Canadian dollar.

In addition to giving you easy access to the upward movement in these currencies, these accounts will pay a monthly dividend if the interest rates of the Canadian or the Australian dollar are high enough. In this way, these currency ETFs act much like a fixed income investment (or a bond mutual fund) but they are denominated in Canadian or Australian dollars. Because of this, they will move up and down according to the market, sometimes as much as 1–2 percent per day or greater.

Currency ETFs can be a great way to get into the commodities area of investing while getting a monthly cash dividend at the same time. As with all investments, when there is a dividend, the risks of the investment are minimized. If a currency ETF pays 4 percent per year in dividends, for example, the investment can go down 4 percent that year and you would still be in a breakeven status.

If you consider these two ETFs—FXA and FXC—for your investments, keep in mind the raw materials that these countries produce: gold and metals in Australia, and grains, gold, and oil in Canada. Even if you are more traditional in your commodities investments and are buying gold coins, oil ETFs, or grain futures, adding the income and diversification of commodity currency ETFs can add diversity to your investment portfolio.

CTAs, TSX, and Private Placements

On the farthest end of indirect commodities investing lies the exotic world of commodities trading advisors (CTAs), buying private placements, and going to the Toronto Stock Exchange (TSX) to buy your penny stocks.

These three areas are complex investments, but they can offer great returns. *CTA*s, commodities trading advisors, are private money managers who specialize in futures trading. After the selection process, your CTA will accept your cash deposit and then trade your account on your behalf. He usually will charge a percentage of money managed plus a percentage of the profits.

Commodities trading advisors will help you choose an investment objective from several trading schemes. If you are interested in finding and using a CTA, it is best to do your research, as there can be long lockup times (commitment periods) and high minimums required. This means that some managers only take clients with a $25,000 minimum investment, for example, and a six- to twelve-month lockup period during which the money can't be returned to the investor.

The stocks that are listed on the **Toronto Stock Exchange (TSX)** are mainly commodities based. This exchange lists copper companies, oil companies, and other commodities companies that are too small to be listed on large exchanges. In addition to the fact that these companies are smaller, the stocks are often low in price, sometimes only a few dollars or less. These are often called **penny stocks** and represent one of the most risky types of commodities investing. A typical company in this exchange is a startup commodities company that is raising cash to begin business operations. It might have geological studies, suppliers, and buyers lined up but is not yet into production. These stocks can be the "wild card" of your commodities investments: you could buy hundreds of shares in such a company for the price of only 10 shares of an established commodities company.

If you keep in mind that often these startup companies are new and not yet in production, and you accept the risk that such companies may remain undiscovered, then you can "salt" your investment portfolio with some of these TSX stocks. At the same time, some of the best mining companies are listed on the TSX. These mining companies are already producing and offer a good risk/reward ratio. If you are interested in getting into these types of stocks, your online or full-service brokerage should be able to allow you to purchase them in your account.

The last way to invest in commodities is with a private placement. **Private placements** are a form of business agreement in which a commodities company sells interest in itself to a small number of investors. These investments are usually purchased through an investment bank because there is a certain level of regulation and compliance that goes into the offering.

FACT

An example in which a private placement might work well would be with an independent oil driller based in Oklahoma. The driller would have all of the research and geo-studies finished, as well as have suppliers for his drilling equipment on the line. He would also have a good management staff and an accurate estimate of the daily barrel production of the wells. Lastly, he would have a sales agreement in place for the crude that the wells will produce when completed and producing.

The investment bank would estimate the value of the wells and production, and divide the small enterprise into shares. Each share would be sold to investors for a set price in exchange for a percentage ownership in the business and a claim to future profits. In this case, it would be typical for a share to cost $50,000 and the total capital raise necessary to be less than $20 million. These types of capital raises are perfect for private placements or a small capital raise on the Toronto Stock Exchange. In addition to a listing on the TSX, the investment bank might arrange to have an option or warrant against the earnings of the company listed on a derivative friendly exchange such as the Frankfurt, Germany exchange.

CHAPTER 20

Making a Go at Commodities Investing

When you decide to begin trading in commodities, you will have to decide whether you are going to be a short-term holder or a long-term investor in raw materials. In addition to keeping good records of your trades for tax purposes, you should keep on the lookout for the feelings of euphoria that can go along with winning big in the commodities market. This chapter will tie together what you've learned so far by talking about profits and emotions.

Short-Term Trading and Long-Term Investing

You must decide if you would like to be a short-term trader or a long-term investor. There are merits to both, but each requires different skill sets and different temperaments. Your first instinct may be that you would like to build up your account slowly and put small amounts into a commodity mutual fund. You may also decide that you would like to take your time building up a pool of knowledge about all of the different pieces that go into the commodities trading puzzle. You may be taking a class in night school that discusses some of the economic indicators that are discussed in this book. You may also find that you would like to join an investment club, or to invest with your entire family as a group. If this were the case, you would certainly need to accumulate shares of commodities mutual funds and ETFs slowly, and only after being very sure of your decisions.

If you do not want to feel the pressure and stress of trading but you still like the idea of owning commodities, then you can take it slow and build up your position over time. You may find the process of buying your favorite commodity over weeks, months, and years to be very rewarding. Sometimes it is the accumulation of the commodity ETF, bag of pennies, or gold coins that gives you a sense of accomplishment.

You may even feel a sense of well-being when you know that you have been dollar cost averaging into an oil-and-gas specialty mutual fund with every paycheck. You might also feel a sense of being almost lucky that you had the foresight to begin buying the shares of this mutual fund at the end of the driving season last year, right after Labor Day as this time of the year is considered the end of the driving season, creating lessening demand, and lessening interest from traders (who might otherwise be bidding up the price of oil and therefore driving up the price of the oil stocks!)

ALERT

It might be interesting if you keep track of the quality and accuracy of your information sources by keeping those brokers' reports on file. Look back on them every three to six months to see if what they predicted would happen actually did happen when they said it would!

Going long term adds a certain amount of stability to your portfolio also, as the commodities market will naturally move up and down from week to week. At the same time, if you are long term, you can enjoy taking your time and picking the best deals in the market.

If you feel strongly or if there is a lot of data suggesting that copper will rise to $4.75 per pound during the next economic expansion, then you will have a period of five to seven years to build up your position in the metal. You might take this time to get into a copper ETF as well as a few of the smaller copper mining companies that may be listed on the Toronto Stock Exchange. You might also have your grandkids sort through pennies when they visit you in order to build up your physical holdings of copper by hording 1982 and older U.S. pennies.

The secret is that when you are a long-term investor you have the benefit of having time on your side. You can sit out a rough patch in the commodities market, when oil is exploding in price and you've missed the ride in price. You may want to sit out a whole season if you are buying any of the raw materials that go up during certain times of the year. This means that if you are a "gold bug" and are building a long-term holding in gold and silver, then you may want to not buy any gold during the height of the gold season, December through March. You will know that oil gets expensive after Memorial Day and continues at its lofty prices until the end of summer and kids go back to school in the fall.

If you are a long-term investor, you can be extra patient and get your commodities investments when the time and price is best for you.

Record Keeping and Taxes

Keeping good records of what you have bought and sold is 95 percent of the battle of maintaining your commodities trading venture as a business. There are two basic ways to run your commodities operation. The first is that you are running it as a business, with expenses, income, and costs of investments. In this case you would treat your buying and selling of leveraged ETF, futures, and mutual funds with the idea that the whole endeavor was done for a profit, as a business.

This means that you would be able to deduct most of your expenses including the cost of your Internet service, your iPad, and periodicals on the form of your income tax return that is designed for profit or loss from a small business.

In your income tax return, you will need to consult your tax advisor, accountant, or attorney, but basically you have the choice of making your trading business as a proprietary, which means you are running your trading as a trading business. If you chose this route, you would have different tax forms to fill out rather than if you were trading for yourself on a personal account. Again, consult your tax advisor to see what method of setting up your trading endeavors is best for your tax situation, as the IRS has complex regulations and rules for both.

ESSENTIAL

Always seek the help of a tax professional when you are filing your trading income tax returns, especially for the first time. If you have traded for the entire year, you will have many records to go through and many gains and losses. A tax professional can help you sort through the paperwork and know what the legal requirements are for filing tax returns on your investment gains.

If you decide to establish your trading as a business or proprietary, you most likely will have many buys and sells, and few expenses relating to the cost of doing business. For example, if you were into trading the same handful of oil, corn, and soybean ETFs for the entire year, you will need to keep track of each trade.

This means that you must keep track of the day, hour, number of units, as well as the price of the ETF. When the ETF is sold minutes, days, or weeks later, you would match up the number of units bought with the number of units sold. In other words, each trade should be recorded as a buy and then matched to those units as they are sold. This really helps at tax time, as there are regulations as to determining the gains made on each trade in the order in which they are made during the year.

This sounds easy but can be tricky as you may have built up a position of a copper ETF or stock over a long time. It may mean that you have ten (or more) smaller trades of 10 units each that go into the entire position of 100 units that later were sold at different times, but the lot size of each sell wasn't a perfect match as what they were when they were bought (the first sell may be 20 units, the second sell 5 units, the third sell 22 units, etc.)

If this happens to you, you will need to use the **first-in**, **first-out method** of accounting. This accounting method shows that the first groups of stocks or ETFs that are sold are matched up in number to the first group of ETFs that are priced at one price point that were bought. To explain it further, if you bought 100 XYZ at $75 and 100 XYZ a week later at $85, and then a month later you sold 125 shares of XYZ at $90, then 100 shares of XYZ would be matched up with the first group (bought at $75) and therefore have a profit of $15 ($90 − $75 = $15).

And the remaining 25 shares sold would be matched up with the second group and therefore have a profit of $5 ($90 − $85 = $5).

Keep in mind that this type of recording may be taken care of by your broker. It might be a good thing when shopping for a broker to ask if the brokerage firm offers this service called **cost basis service**. Cost basis service is a book keeping service that does this first in first out matching of the trades in-house on their computers. If so, you will be sent a report at the end of the year with all of the work done for you; these reports are usually accepted by the IRS. If not, and you have kept good records, you should have no problem when it comes time to pay the taxes on your gains.

If you don't keep good records, and the brokerage firm you are using does not offer cost basis calculation, then at the end of the year you will be sent a form that lists only the gains in the account and will leave out any costs associated with the purchase of the stock or ETF.

In other words, if you bought and sold $50,000 worth of ETFs, mutual funds, or stock but you spent $40,000 buying them, then you have a gain of $10,000. If the broker doesn't keep records as to cost basis, and you don't have records, the IRS will be sent a form at the end of the year that states you had gains of $50,000! With this information, the IRS will bill you for the tax on the entire $50,000. Clearly you wouldn't want to pay this full tax. Therefore it would be best to keep good records.

The Emotions of Trading Commodities

Once you've earned money from trading commodities you will have the special feeling that money made in the markets can be very empowering. Placing a trade in your account and then waiting for it to turn around and show a profit can seem to add time to your life. In other words, each and every moment that you will be waiting for the commodities you bought to turn, you most likely will be experiencing a heightened state of being wide awake. Having money in a trade and then following the trade on CNBC, Kitco.com, or Bloomberg can give you a sense of euphoria when the trade completes its run and you close it out at a profit.

Experiencing high returns on a leveraged ETF trade or in futures trading can make you walk around with a certain smile on your face. This comes from making the efforts to take control of your life through trading. It seems silly, but if you have made a certain amount of money from your trading that has been set aside for additional trading in more commodities, then there is a certain control that comes from this kind of budgeting.

Not only this, but you will feel a kinship with all of those who are on the news stations reporting what has happened at this or that central bank. You will feel that you are more connected to the investing world—as if what happens in China and in the European Central Bank does actually affect you. You will notice the price changes of the commodities move up and down according to the news, and you will begin to see and feel that your finances are integrated into the well-being of the world.

This feeling of integration with the world can be the beginning of a lifetime of study, investing, and excitement for you or for those you choose to discuss you're trading with. There are many people today who live somewhat in a bubble, with a smaller-than-necessary view of the world. These often are the people who work all day in an office and then go to the mall on the weekend. They might spend some time at a coffee shop discussing politics with their friends.

Wouldn't their lives be more fully enriched with the study of the money supplies and economies of the world's largest economies? Even if these same people like to think of themselves as "counterculture," would they do well to think of themselves in a larger context that involves the growth rates of China, the oil output of Norway, and the economic situation of the euro currency member states?

QUESTION

How do you know when you are enjoying too much the risk aspect of trading?
You will know when you are feeling giddy in the pit of your stomach or thrilled with how much margin you are using or how much money you have on the line. Risk is like a drug, and it can be quite addictive! If you feel these emotions, watch out!

You may find that your study of commodities trading has led you to a place of greater understanding of how the economic world works. You may want to progress further in your studies and read all you can about money, banking, and finance. If you do so, then you will be joining a select group of people who throughout history have studied these subjects and used their knowledge to help plan for and build their own and sometimes their country's wealth base.

Success's Highs and Failure's Lows

Making a capital gain in the market, or making a gain from trading commodities, can lead to a feeling of euphoria. After a series of trading wins it can seem as though you are invincible, and that your precision in analytics, strategy, and execution of trades has created "something from nothing"; whereas you once had an account balance of "x amount," you now have an account balance with several hundred or thousands more dollars!

It may seem as though your account is growing like magic, and your interception of the markets has given you an "inside view" as to where the prices of commodities have gone and will be going in the future. If you have been planning your trades, and buying and selling your commodities with gut feelings and logic, then there is a certain amount of truth to this statement. The facts are, if you are going about learning all there is to know about what is discussed on central banking websites; if you are reading through your brokers' reports; and if you are making and studying technical charts, then you are way ahead of most other buyers and sellers of commodities (or any other stock or ETF, for that matter).

The secret to doing well and to being fairly consistent with the returns in your account is not allowing these euphoric feelings to overshadow the fact that you are using a mix of analysis, others' knowledge, and a bit of luck to get your trades to the point where they will bring you profits.

ALERT

Knowing that there is just a tiny bit of luck that goes into every trade will go a long way in helping you keep your wits about you during good times and bad. Luck is with even the best traders! They just "help luck along" with the right amount of analytics, gut feeling, and logic.

This is a key element to consistently gaining in the market: knowing that winning in the market is *not* all your doing. It would be better to remember that there is a lot that goes into a winning trade: opportunity, research, and a bit of luck.

If you are beginning to think that you're winning in the market all on your own doing, then chances are you will soon begin to take more and more risks in order to prove yourself "right" and that you can call the commodities markets' direction and make a perfect trade every time. If this happens to you—if you are feeling that you "understand it all"—then this is the perfect time to step back and walk away from commodities trading. It seems that when a good trader is at the point that she thinks she "understands it all," she will begin to place trades that are more and more haphazard in nature. The underlying feeling is that because she "knows more" that she can skip steps in fundamental and technical analysis and go right to the business of buying and selling the raw materials of her choice without the proper time to think the trade through.

There are always stories of the big banks having traders who have gone rogue, who have built up huge positions in one side of a trade. Then these trades continue to get worse and worse, and with leverage and margin, the trader builds up more and more of the investment. The process can go on for months at a time, with the trader covering his tracks and covering his losses with false gains. He is a ***rogue trader*** and when he is finished, the losses can be in the billions!

Being your own boss and trading for your own account, it can be just as easy for you to cover your losses with more built-upon trades. If you find yourself getting to the point where you know it all, or even more so, the market isn't "acting right" and you begin to "force" your trades, then this is the time to step back, take a breather, and steer clear of the markets for a while.

The commodities markets can be easy to learn, but just when they seem to give you profits with ease, they can seem to take it all away and get you in a situation in which you are expecting gains each time but they don't seem to be coming!

If you are in this situation, you are in a rut, and you are suffering from hubris, or what is called the winner's curse—overconfidence in your ability. This is common amongst beginning mid-level traders. If you are getting to this point, walk away from trading, cool off, and get back to it when the time feels right.

The Law of the Opposites

This discussion of the winner's curse brings up another of the key elements to trading in general. This is the law of "do the opposite of what you feel." One of the crucial elements to learning how to trade effectively is to get to the point where you are trading with a cold, calculating efficiency. This means that you will scan the news, read your brokers' reports, and analyze the technical indicators with a certain iciness that would go if you were breaking down your successes with precision.

With this in mind, be warned that sometimes the emotions of trading can also lead you to a place where there is a clear path that can be taken, but your thoughts are against it. For example, it may be that the price of crude oil has risen 15 percent in the past two weeks. This price might have gone up due to geopolitical problems in one of the oil-producing countries of the Middle East, which has caused a hotspot of activity in crude-oil trading. You may know, and your ideas have been seconded by traders quoted on CNBC, that the country with the geopolitical problem has such low oil-production that even if this nation totally stopped producing oil it wouldn't affect supply by much.

It would seem as though your ideas as to the trade would be logically based. In fact, it is an obvious trade: short the oil market with a 3× bear oil ETF. As you read this book and see the obvious nature of the trade, it may be very difficult for you to place the trade to short the oil market when the price has spiked by so much. In fact, you might be tempted to sit the market out and wait for it all to blow over, or you might even be tempted to get on the long side of the trade and ride the price of oil even higher.

FACT

Doing the opposite of what you feel can be one of the hardest, yet most profitable things to do when trading. On one of the most volatile days in recent history, the S&P 500 went down 10 percent in one day, only to go up 10 percent the next. That would have been a perfect trade for the disciplined investor!

A word of advice when you and the commodities markets are in this situation is to do what is logical and do the opposite of what you feel. If you are at the point that you are thinking, "Oh my, this price is scary, it will never come down," then you are thinking only with emotion and are not using the other tools in your toolkit: logic and planning. Using logic and planning can go a long way in keeping your trades very profitable during bad times, as these bad times (bad news days) can be one of the best times to trade. This is often because the other people in the market are reacting emotionally and are not thinking the whole trade through.

Commodities Trading as a Pastime

You certainly have been presented with a lot of information to digest by reading this book. You now know that investing in commodities can be one of the most rewarding and fun parts of building up your investment portfolio. You know you can trade commodities that are as complex as futures options and leveraged ETFs, all the way down to the oldest and most simple form of investing, which is holding the physical commodity in your hands.

Now that you've read this book, you most likely have a deeper understanding of how adding commodities to an investment portfolio of stocks and bonds can help keep that portfolio well diversified and well balanced.

You most likely have the know-how to read through the news and broker's reports with an eye open for trading ideas. Not only this, but you know that it takes time for an investment cycle to be complete, and that this may mean that the prices of your commodity go up and down in the short term. On the other hand, this is the same reason that you should consider getting into commodities now. Since 2008 the world's economies have just gone through a period of acute stress and rapid slowdown, bringing with it the bottoming of an economic cycle.

This means that you are in a prime period to begin investing and building a position in commodities. This is because commodities are sensitive to good economic conditions. A healthy (or getting healthier) worldwide economy can bring great pressure on the prices of gold, copper, grains, and oil.

If you were to stand and look at the timing of the commodities cycle, you may conclude what many others have: that the world's economies are getting healthier, and thus there is a greater and greater chance of an upcoming boom in the prices of raw materials.

After the main issue of learning how commodities can be an integral part of your investment scheme, you have also been exposed to how to perform fundamental and technical analysis. This, along with the added groundwork of monitoring the economy, central banking, growth, and money supply should leave you with a well-balanced idea of how you can go about turning your commodities trading endeavors into your commodities trading pastime.

APPENDIX A

Glossary

200-day moving average

A technical indicator that uses a rolling average of the last 200 days' closing balances as its data points. It produces a gently sloping line against the bar chart.

Actual gold weight (AGW), actual silver weight (ASW)

The percentage content of the coin or bar that is pure gold or silver after the alloys have been removed. Used for measurement only, as the coins and bars are not actually melted down.

Advising firm

A brokerage firm that offers an electronic trading platform, record keeping, and personal advice, as opposed to a discount broker, which only offers the platform.

Alternative assets class

A class of assets that is separate from stocks, cash, and bonds.

AUD

The currency of Australia, the Australian dollar.

Bar chart

A technical chart that uses bars to represent the upward and downward movement of commodities' prices during a set time frame.

Base metals

See industrial metals

Bear fund

An ETF that is set up to make a profit when the commodity's price goes down in value.

Bull fund

An ETF that is set up to make a profit when the commodity's price goes up in price.

Bullion

A term that refers to physical precious metals that are in coin or bar form (as opposed to jewelry form).

Brokers' reports

The research reports that are issued by brokers to help their clients make educated trades.

Bubble

A point at which the price of an asset gets too high to support itself, and so it then reverses.

Candlestick chart

A form of technical chart that uses colored bars with tails to graphically display the asset's up and down price movements.

Capital gains

Income that is made by trading, as opposed to income made from working.

Capital preservation

The goal of keeping assets in an account safe with little risk, on a daily basis.

Central bank

A bank, or banks, for a country or economic zone that also sets interest rates and helps control the speed of the economy through money supply.

Central banking stance

The direction that a central bank is going in with its monitoring and acting on the economy in the next six to twelve months.

Chinese New Year

A major holiday in Asia that has gold buying as its tradition.

Commodities

Raw materials that go into the building and producing of manufactured goods.

Commodities trading advisor (CTA)

A money manager who specializes in commodities futures and commodities futures options.

Commodity company stock

A share of common stock in a company that mines, grows, drills for, or is related to the procurement of raw materials.

Commodity currency

The currency of a country that has commodities exports as one of its main sources of income, such as the New Zealand dollar, Australian dollar, Canadian dollar, and Norwegian kroner.

Commodity index ETF

An ETF that is set up to track the value of one of the well-known commodities indexes.

Commodity mutual fund

A mutual fund that has as its primary investment objective to invest in commodity related stocks, precious metal bullion, or commodity futures.

CTA

See commodities trading advisor

Diversification

The investing concept of not putting all of your eggs in one basket; putting your assets in as many asset classes as possible to prevent downturns.

Dollar index

The value of the U.S. dollar relative to the value against a basket of foreign currencies.

Dr. Copper

The name given to copper because movement in copper price is a reliable indicator of the direction of the world's economies. The common joke is that Dr. Copper has a PhD in economics.

Dry powder

Cash reserves kept on hand to be readily available when buying opportunities arise.

Electronic spot trading

Trading that is without leverage, in an electronic format, and directly tied to the price of the commodity.

Electronic traded fund (ETF)

An investment that holds a basket of assets like a mutual fund, but which is traded during the day like a stock.

Entire investment universe

Refers to all of the possible investments that are available to an investor.

ETF

See Electronic traded fund

Federal Reserve System (the Fed)

The central bank of the United States.

Fineness

A number in 1000ths that defines the purity of the gold or silver in a coin or bar. Example: a pre-1964 U.S. quarter is 0.900 fine, or 90 percent silver and 10 percent nonprecious metal.

First-in first-out method

An accounting method that matches up the sale of securities in the same order in which they were bought, with the cost of the earliest shares matched with the sales price of the first sold shares.

Forex

Short for "foreign exchange market," the forex is also called the currency market.

Fractional gold or fractional gold coins

Gold coins that are of Actual Gold Weights that are not of the usual $1/_{10}$-, $1/_4$-, $1/_2$-, or 1-ounce size. These are usually antique European and Asian gold coins that were used as actual money before 1949. Common weights are .2354 ounce gold for the British Sovereign, and .1867 ounce gold for the French 20 Franc Rooster.

Freely interchangeable

Each unit of a particular commodity is freely interchangeable with another unit of the same commodity.

Fully interchangeable

The requirement that the underlying of a futures is exchangeable in quality with each other underlying. *Same as freely interchangable.*

Fundamental analysis

The study of the bigger picture of trading, such as the economic trends, interest rates, and other longer-term indicators as to the condition of the economy as it relates to commodities trading.

Futures options

Options that are traded and priced exactly like options on stocks (the common form) but are options on futures. Their price will move up and down on the up and down of the price of the future contract that they are tied to, not to a stock like a stock option. In all other aspects, such as the complex time element of their pricing and trading strategies, futures options are the same as stock options.

GLD

An ETF that follows the price of gold.

Going long

A trade that will make money when the market goes up.

Good delivery bars

A term that refers to the a certain grade fineness and authorized manu-facturer of precious metals bars that are high enough quality to be used to fulfill a precious metals futures contract if the contract holder asked for delivery of the actual metal (as opposed to just settling in cash.)

Hedge fund

An investment that is unregulated and is able to use leverage to amplify its returns beyond the normal returns of the market.

Hedger

One who enters into a futures contract with a business purpose that relates to her actual need for the underlying in the futures contract. An example is an airline company manager who buys oil futures to hedge the price of jet fuel that the airlines will use six months in the future.

Industrial metals

The commodities metals that are related to building and manufacturing.

Ingots

Bars of physical metal that weigh from 1 gram to 1,000 ounces each.

Lagging indicators

Fundamental data that is revealed after the events have already happened.

Leading indicator

Fundamental data that is revealed before the events have happened.

Leveraged 2× or 3× index ETF

An ETF that uses margin to amplify its returns either two or three times.

Load

The pricing structure of mutual funds equivalent to the sales charge or commission of the fund. (As opposed to no-load funds, which have no sales charge or commissions.)

Managed futures

A type of investment fund that is run by a professional and is invested in commodities futures.

Margin call

When your futures broker automatically closes out your account because your losses are too great and your equity in the account has fallen below a minimum level.

Melt value

See actual gold weight (AGW)

Mispricing

When a commodity is priced too high or too low relative to its value.

Money supply

The quantity as to the amount of cash, coin, checking, savings, and money markets both onshore and overseas.

Mutual funds

An investment that pools investors' resources and then diversifies them within an asset class.

Natural resources

Raw materials.

NYMEX

New York Mercantile Exchange

Penny stocks

A stock that is too small or too low a share price to be listed on a larger exchange. Usually considered to be higher risk.

Physical commodity

The actual commodity that is being traded (the barrel of oil, bushel of corn, etc.), not the futures contract itself.

Portfolio theory

The investment theory that a well-diversified portfolio will perform better and at less risk than a portfolio that is concentrated in one or two assets.

Price discovery

The process of knowing how much your goods or securities (mutual funds, futures, or ETFs) are worth both at the buying point and at the present.

Private placements

A type of equity investment that is sold in shares like a stock, but the company is usually very small; therefore, there are a smaller number of shares available for investors, usually at a higher share price than a usual stock. Most private placements are sold in units with a price tag of $25,000 or higher, and are only sold to high net worth investors.

Proprietary trading firm

Trading houses are set up like partnerships, where each trader buys in to the ownership of the firm and therefore shares with the profits of all of the other owners/traders.

Pyramiding

The trading theory that you should buy into the position in thirds, and then sell off in thirds. This process reduces risk.

Quantitative easing

The process by which a central bank loosens the money supply by a series of measures including the buying of assets, which puts more money into circulation.

Rogue trader

A trader in an investment bank who works for the bank but is compensated with a bonus that is tied to the gains on his trades. The rogue trader will over-trade his account in order to earn a higher bonus, but when the trades turn to a loss, he will cover up the losing trades with false trades. This scheme will go on until the losses are too big to cover up with false trades.

Setup

The best time to buy or sell your commodity; that is, conditions are right to get in to a particular trade with a good chance of making a profit.

Soft commodities

The technical name for food commodities.

Speculator

One who enters into a futures contract for the express purpose of making capital gains but has no need for the underlying of the futures contract for business purposes.

Spot price

Called the cash price by some traders. This is the cash and carry price, the price of the commodity at the market, paid for in full at immediate delivery, as opposed to a futures price, which is the price of the commodity at a future delivery date.

Strong buy order

When a brokerage house tells its clients to buy an asset.

Tactical allocation

The process of changing the composition of your trading portfolio with a short term timeframe according to market conditions.

Technical analysis

The process of timing the buys and sells of a commodity by looking at charts of lines and wavy lines—that is, estimated price direction charted over time (wavy lines) compared with the actual direction of trends over time (vertical straight line).

Time premium

The element of an options price that is related to the length of time the contract is good for before expiring. For example, if the option has sixty days left before expiring, there is a complex formula that gives value to these sixty days in dollar terms and adds it to the price of the option. On the next day, the option is good for one day less, or fifty-nine days. The formula would calculate the "time premium" to be worth one day less in dollar terms, and on until the time value was zero when the option expired on the 59th day.

Trading market risk or growth

The process of setting up trades that make money according to the risk appetite of the world's investors.

Uncorrelated

When an asset's price goes up and down unrelated of a second asset's movement in price.

Underlying

The commodity that the futures contract bases its price on. For example, each mini-wheat future contract has 1,000 bushels of #2 wheat as its underlying.

Value stocks

A term that refers to stocks that pay large dividends in relation to their share price.

Waiting for the trough

The same thing as "buying on the dips" with the added notion of waiting for a slowing of the momentum of a commodity's price movement.

Year-on-year comparison

A comparison between the current month or quarter and the same period from the previous year (also called a year-over-year comparison).

APPENDIX B

Additional Resources

Books

Bernstein, Peter L. *The Power of Gold: The History of an Obsession.* (New York: John Wiley & Sons, 2000).

Bernstein, Peter L. *Against the Gods: The Remarkable Story of Risk.* (New York: John Wiley & Sons, 1998).

Burgess, Gareth A. *Trading and Investing in the Forex Market Using Chart Techniques.* (Chichester, West Sussex, UK: John Wiley & Sons, 2009).

Downes, John, and Jordan Elliot Goodman. *Finance & Investment Handbook.* (Hauppauge, NY: Barron's Educational Series, 2010).

Ferguson, Niall. *The House of Rothschild, Volumes 1 and 2.* (New York: Penguin Books, 1999, 2000).

Gilbert, Richard E., Tom Engle, and Cooksey Shugart. *Complete Price Guide to Watches 2012.* (Mount Pleasant, SC: Tinderbox Press, 2011). *Shows detailed illustrations of gold-filled, 14-karat gold, and sterling silver hallmarks.*

News Sources

Barron's

http://online.barrons.com

CNBC

www.cnbc.com

DailyStocks

www.dailystocks.com

The Economist

www.economist.com

Federal Reserve Bank of New York

www.newyorkfed.org
www.newyorkfed.org/research/directors_charts/econ_fin.pdf

Moody's Analytics

www.economy.com

The Motley Fool

www.fool.com

MSN Money

http://moneycentral.msn.com/investor/home.asp

Oanda Forex Trading

www.oanda.com

The Wall Street Journal

www.wallstreetjournal.com

Yahoo! Finance

http://finance.yahoo.com

Websites for Fundamental Analysis Research

Bank of England

www.bankofengland.co.uk

Bank for International Settlements

www.bis.org

Central Bank Website Listings

http://www.bis.org/cbanks.htm

Bank of Japan

www.boj.or.jp/en

CME Group

www.cmegroup.com

Deutsche Bank USA

www.db.com/usa

European Central Bank

www.ecb.int

InvestorsEurope

www.investorseurope.com

Kitco Base Metals

www.kitcometals.com

Kitco Gold & Precious Metals

www.kitco.com

Kitco Silver

www.kitcosilver.com

The London Bullion Market Association

www.lbma.org.uk

London Metal Exchange

www.lme.com

Merrill Lynch International

www.ml.com

Monetary Authority of Singapore

www.mas.gov.sg

Norges Bank (Norway)

www.norges-bank.no

OANDA fxTrade

http://fxtrade.oanda.com

Reserve Bank of Australia

www.rba.gov.au

Reserve Bank of New Zealand

www.rbnz.govt.nz

The Riksbank

www.riksbank.com

SW Consulting SA

Directory of Swiss banks

http://www.swconsult.ch

Stock, Futures, and Options

www.sfomag.com

The Swiss National Bank

www.snb.ch

UBS Global Homepage

www.ubs.com

U.S. Bureau of Economic Analysis

www.bea.gov

U.S. Department of the Treasury

www.ustreas.gov

U.S. Federal Reserve System

www.federalreserve.gov

World Gold Council

www.gold.org

Keyword Searches for the Internet

"gold coin weights"

"gold coin dealers"

"gold dealers *your zip code*"

"coin dealers *your zip code*"

"oil and gas investment banks"

"copper stocks"

"gold and silver penny stocks"

"energy mutual funds"

"oil and gas mutual funds"

"commodity mutual funds"

"listing of leveraged ETFs"

"dr. copper"

"commodity currency"

"commodity trading advisor *your zip code*"

"New Zealand's natural resources"

"Australia's natural resources"

"Canada's natural resources"

"How to buy Toronto Stock Exchange stocks"

APPENDIX C

Futures Trading Screenshots

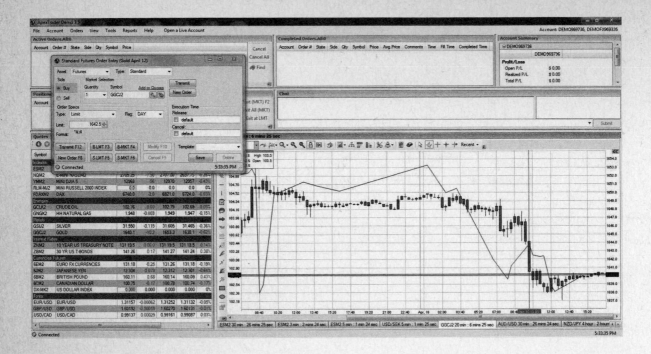

This is a screenshot of a Futures Order Entry screen showing a Buy order for a Gold Futures contract.

This is a screenshot of the Trading Platform from Apex Futures *www.apexfutures.com/trading-platforms/apextrader/?ref=CRDB* showing Fibonacci lines on a Gold Futures contract chart. You can see that the Fibonacci line group is drawn from the low part of the curve and is traced with the highest line in the Fibonacci group to the highest part of the upward slope. From this, you can see that the price of the gold future (and the chart) falls until it reaches the bottom-most line in the Fibonacci line. At this point, the downward trend is in reversal and begins to move upward.

This is a screenshot of the Trading Platform showing a close up of the Fibonacci lines drawn on a Gold futures contract.

This is a screen shot of the Trading Platform from Apex Futures *www.apexfutures.com/ trading-platforms/apextrader/?ref=CRDB* showing a buy order of 5 lots of 1,000 units each of the New Zealand dollar against the Japanese yen (NZD/JPY.) The "order boxes" are shown as are the number of lots to "buy." In addition to this is shown a New Zealand dollar to Japanese yen (NZD/JPY) chart showing the fact that the New Zealand dollar has gone down against the Japanese yen (downward slope on chart) and is set to go up in value. This is a trade that would be placed if there was news that the price of the soft commodities were rising or if there was talk about added demand of food and related commodities throughout Asia. This news might be due to a report of a strong economy in China, for example.

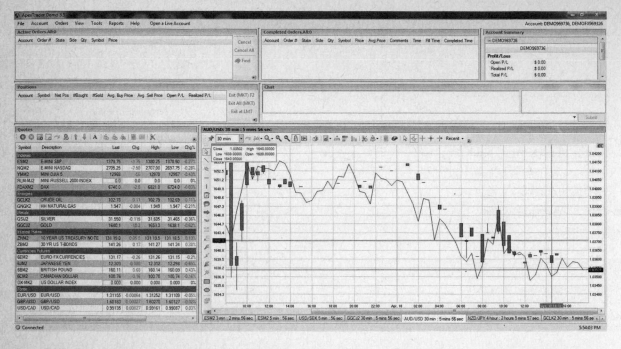

This is a screen shot showing the correlation between the price of the Australian dollar and the price of gold (as shown through the price of the gold futures contract.) The time frames and scales are the same for both. The Australian dollar is shown in a line that has peaks and valleys and looks like a mountain range. On top of this chart is drawn the gold futures contract. You can see here that the Australian dollar (AUD/USD) is going up and down and follows very closely the price of gold futures contract, shown by the vertical lines of the candlestick chart. This chart acts as a back up to the idea that the AUD/USD currency trade will move up with the price of gold. With this in mind, you could buy AUD/USD forex contracts or the Australian dollar ETF "FXA" to track a gold trading position.

This is a screen shot showing the correlation between the gold futures contract and the crude oil futures contract. The gold futures contract is shown with a line that has peaks and valleys with the look of a mountain range. It is shown up against the crude oil futures contract with the same timeframe and scale, shown in a candlestick chart. You can see that the price of gold moves upward and downward in a similar direction to the price of crude oil (as shown by their futures contracts).

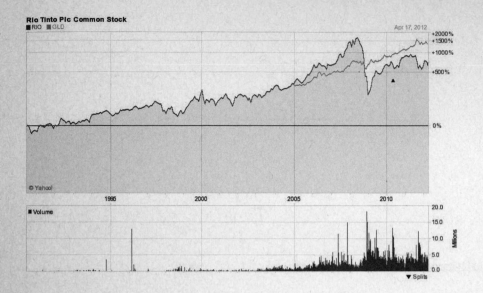

Rio Tinto Plc Common Stock
RIO GLD

Apr 17, 2012

+2000%
+1500%
+1000%
+500%
0%

© Yahoo!

1995   2000   2005   2010

Volume

20.0
15.0
10.0
5.0
0.0

Millions

▼ Splits

This is a chart showing the correlation between the price of Rio Tinto common stock "RIO" and the gold ETF "GLD". You can see the impressive returns of the ETF for bullion gold and the equally impressive returns of the international mining company Rio Tinto.

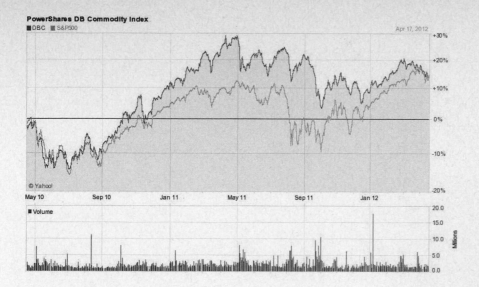

This is a chart comparing the returns of the U.S. stock market represented by the S & P 500 and the DBC Commodities Index ETF. The Commodities Index has positive returns while the S & P 500 has losses.

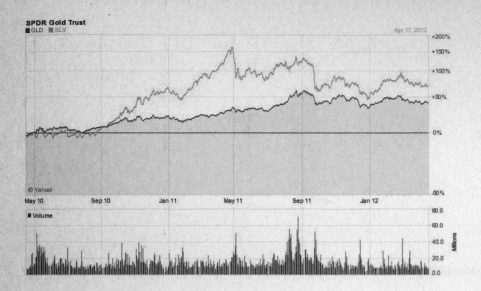

This chart shows the correlation between the gold ETF "GLD" and the returns of the silver ETF "SLV." As you can see, in general, the price of silver (represented by the share price of SLV) moves up with the price of gold (represented by the share price of GLD). Often times the movement of silver will be more substantial than the price movement of gold in the same timeframe. This is shown by the higher highs and the lower lows of the percentage of returns of the two precious metals.

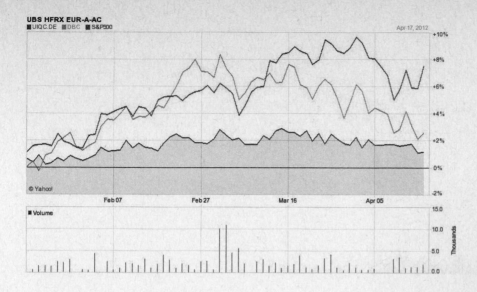

This is perhaps the most complex chart, showing the relationship over a one-year time period of three indexes: an alternative asset index (represented by the UBS Hedge Fund Index "UIQG.DE") the bottom line, the S & P 500 Index, and the DBC Commodities Index ETF (DBC) the middle line. With this chart, you can see that within the alternative asset category, a common commodities index is up 15+ percent while a common hedge fund index is down 7 percent in the same timeframe. You can also see that the daily returns of the U.S. stock market (S & P 500) oftentimes move inversely to the returns of the commodities index. This is a good example of the diversification effect of adding commodities to your portfolio, whereby the value of your commodities investments would move up when the price of your equities (stock) investments were moving down.

INDEX

We Have
EVERYTHING
on Anything!

With more than 19 million copies sold, **the Everything® series** has become one of America's favorite resources for solving problems, learning new skills, and organizing lives. Our brand is not only recognizable—it's also welcomed.

The series is a hand-in-hand partner for people who are ready to tackle new subjects—like you!

For more information on the Everything® series, please visit *www.adamsmedia.com*

The Everything® list spans a wide range of subjects, with more than 500 titles covering 25 different categories:

Business	History	Reference
Careers	Home Improvement	Religion
Children's Storybooks	Everything Kids	Self-Help
Computers	Languages	Sports & Fitness
Cooking	Music	Travel
Crafts and Hobbies	New Age	Wedding
Education/Schools	Parenting	Writing
Games and Puzzles	Personal Finance	
Health	Pets	